LIFE IN ANNWN

The Story of Willy Jones' Afterlife

by

Owen Jones

Life In Annwn

Copyright

Published by Megan Publishing Services
Copyright © Owen Jones 2025
https://meganpublishingservices.com/

ISBN: 978-1-0683538-4-0

All Rights Reserved

DISCLAIMER:

This novel is a work of fiction. Names, characters, businesses, places, events, and incidents are either the product of the author's imagination or used in a fictitious manner. Any resemblance to actual persons, living or dead, or actual events is purely coincidental.

The author has made every effort to portray the characters, settings, and events in this book accurately and in a manner consistent with the storyline. However, creative liberties may have been taken for the sake of the narrative.

Readers are reminded that the characters and events depicted in this novel are entirely fictional, and any similarities to real individuals, whether living or deceased, or actual occurrences are unintentional.

The author and publisher disclaim any liability, loss, or risk incurred as a consequence, directly or indirectly, of the use and application of any contents of this novel. Any resemblance to persons, living or dead, events, or locales is entirely coincidental.

The Annwn - Heaven Series

Annwn can be seen as the ancient Welsh word for Heaven, although Annwn was underground – or even under the mountains. This led early Christian missionaries from around the Mediterranean to think that they were satanists and devil-worshippers.

A Night in Annwn
The Strange Story of Old Willy Jones' NDE

-

Life in Annwn
The Story of Willy Jones' Life in Heaven

-

Leaving Annwn
Returning to Earth on a Mission!

Contact Details

BlueSky: owen-author.bsky.social
Facebook: AngunJones
Instagram: owen_author
LinkedIn: owencerijones
Pinterest: owen_author
TikTok: @owen_author
X: @owen_author
Blog: Megan Publishing Services

Join our newsletter for insider information
on Owen Jones' books and writing
by adding your email to:
http://meganpublishingservices.com

Inspirational Quotes

Believe not in anything simply because you have heard it,

Believe not in anything simply because it was spoken and rumoured by many,

Believe not in anything simply because it was found written in your religious texts,

Believe not in anything merely on the authority of teachers and elders,

Believe not in traditions because they have been handed down for generations,

But after observation and analysis, if anything agrees with reason and is conducive to the good and benefit of one and all, accept it and live up to it.

Gautama Buddha

Great Spirit, whose voice is on the wind, hear me.
Let me grow in strength and knowledge.
Make me ever behold the red and purple sunset.
May my hands respect the things you have given me.
Teach me the secrets hidden under every leaf and stone, as you have taught people for ages past.
Let me use my strength, not to be greater than my brother, but to

fight my greatest enemy – myself.

Let me always come before you with clean hands and an open heart, that as my Earthly span fades like the sunset, my Spirit shall return to you without shame.

(Based on a traditional **Sioux prayer**)

"I do not seek to walk in the footsteps of the Wise People of old; I seek what they sought".
Matsuo Basho

Myself when young did eagerly frequent
Doctor and Saint, and heard great Argument
About it and about; but oft-times
Came out, by the same Door as in I went.
Omar Khayyam
The Rubaiyat XXIX.

Owen Jones

Contents

LIFE IN ANNWN..
Copyright..ii
The Annwn - Heaven Series..iii
Contact Details..iv
Inspirational Quotes..v
Contents..vii
1. THE FIRST DAY BACK..1
2. A STITCH IN TIME..15
3 PICKING UP A PREVIOUS LIFE..25
4 FINDING A JOB..33
5 GETTING THE BASICS RIGHT..41
6 THE SURFACE..51
7 FAMILY AND OLD FRIENDS..59
8 INCREASING INVOLVEMENT..67
9 HOLIDAYS..75
10 MEETING OLD FRIENDS..85
11 FAMILY..95
12 THE SPIRIT OF CO-OPERATION..103
13 THE BEGINNING..113

14 THE DREAM TAKES FORM	121
15 LOST TREASURE	129
16 A DRAWING BECOMES REALITY	137
17 THE FIRESTONE-EYED CAT	145
Glossary	155
LEAVING ANNWN	157
About the Author	169
Other Books by the Same Author	171

1. THE FIRST DAY BACK

"Whoo-hoo, Sarah! I haven't been on a horse since I was a kid, when Dad used to take me riding on Sunday afternoons after dinner! I'd forgotten how much fun it is. Which way is home, love?"

"All roads lead to home, Willy! It's so nice to see you enjoying yourself, my dear!" replied his wife laughing, her auburn hair flying back in the slipstream as they galloped along on their magnificent black steeds.

"So, over that way, is it?" he asked pointing forward to a spot between two mountains.

"Yes, sure…"

"I thought I recognised it. I've always had a good sense of direction… I've lived in these hills all my life… Same as you, my love, eh?"

"Race you!" she laughed non-committally, and urged her mount on. Willy laughed out loud as he hadn't for several decades and gave chase to the horse that had a slight lead on him.

"Tally Ho!" he shouted as he clenched his horse between his knees and rocked forward. "Tally Ho!" In seconds, he had caught up and he leaned over to shout to his wife, "I don't believe in hunting just for the sake of it, as you know, Sarah, but I wish that those hounds were with us now… The Hounds of Annwn, you called them, didn't you?"

"Yes, my dear, but they are with us. Look behind us". As he stretched around to look, he became aware of seven huge Irish wolf hounds lolloping along just yards behind them. "Wow!" he shouted, "I can't believe I didn't notice them before. This is fantastic! So exhilarating! I feel twenty years younger".

"And you look it too, Willy".

A while later, as they were entering the valley between the two mountains, Willy, leaned over again. "OK, Sarah! Let's call it a draw! We can't be far from home now, but I'm having such a great time that I don't want to go back just yet. Can we stop here and lie on the grass? We can have a chat and play with the dogs while the horses rest a while".

"Sure, we can. Pick a spot".

Willy pulled his mount up within yards, saying, "This'll do right here. The grass looks soft and green, and the view is spectacular". They both dismounted and the dogs swarmed around them. "I didn't realise how tiring riding is until we stopped. My back is starting to ache too…"

"Don't think about it, Willy. You'll be all right in a minute. Come and sit here beside me".

"Don't we have to tether the horses to something?"

"Not really, but we can, if you like… To a sapling? There's one behind you". Willy turned slowly, his hand on the small of his back.

"'s' Funny! I didn't notice that when we rode up".

"Didn't you, dear? Don't worry about it".

Willy tied the reins loosely to the six-foot Rowan, and sat next to his wife. "That's better… much better. I haven't enjoyed myself so much in years. It's great to be with you so much again. I have missed you, you know, since you passed away, or whatever you call it here. I forget now".

"I know, my dear, I know, but I never did leave you, you know. Not really. I was always there".

"But I couldn't see you or touch you".

"Granted, you couldn't touch me, but you could see me sometimes, couldn't you? And you did talk to me… quite often".

"Yes, I suppose I did, but you didn't reply".

"I like to think that you knew what I was saying".

"Yes, I think I did know, looking back on it".

"Yes, I'm sure you did. How is your back now?"

"My? Oh, yes, my back", he said rubbing it. "It's fine. No pain at all. It's just as if I had imagined it". Sarah smiled at him and continued to pet one of the hounds that was nuzzling into her arm.

"They really love you, don't they, those dogs?"

"Yes, and I really love them as well. I can't imagine why people called them the Hounds of Annwn, or Hell, in some cases. They wouldn't hurt a fly".

"Well, they are hunters, and they have to eat, so I suppose they have to do some er… I was going to say 'killing', but I suppose everything here is dead already, so… what do they eat? Talking about food, I'm getting rather peckish myself. I don't suppose you brought any of those sandwiches from my funeral, did you?"

Sarah was looking at him with a quizzical smile as she watched Willy trying to rationalise the situation he found himself in. "If you're hungry, my dear, you will find some sandwiches in my bag". Never liking to look in a lady's bag, even with permission, he put his hand inside and pulled out a large paper bag that felt right. "That's the one", she said. Willy took a few out and offered one to his wife.

"No, thank you, my dear, I rarely eat these days. You could say that I've got out of the habit".

Willy took a bite as she was talking, chewed and stared at her. "We don't need to eat any more, do we?"

"We can, if we want to, but it is not necessarily, no. Some people never realise that though and still eat like they did when they had a body to sustain".

"So, the dogs don't…" Sarah was shaking her head slowly and grinning, "either, so they don't hunt or kill anything…" He looked at the horses, "but the horses are eating the grass!"

"Only because you expect them to…"

"And my back? The same?"

Sarah nodded, smiling as if at a child who had just solved a logical problem. "And look at this", she said retrieving a mirror from her bag without looking.

"I really do look twenty years younger!" he exclaimed brushing his dark hair back with his hands. "And my hair has started growing again!"

"You said that you felt twenty years younger…"

"and so I look it…"

"Yes".

He stopped eating the sandwich and offered it to he nearest dog who took it and swallowed it whole. He looked at Sarah. "You wanted him to… you expected him to, so he did", she said with a shrug. "You can have what you want, as long as people or animals are willing to give it to you, but you can mould the scenery to whatever you want, because that doesn't hurt, can't hurt anyone, since we all see and hear what we want to without it affecting anyone else".

"Doesn't that make conversation rather difficult?"

"Has it with us?"

"No, come to think of it, it hasn't, has it?"

"Well, not for me, no… Nor for you, it seems. However, I choose to be on the same wavelength as you. You haven't really tried talking to anyone else yet, but some won't share with others, or won't try to communicate with people they don't know, but then that's up to them, isn't it? That's the world they choose to live in… some people like people and choose to help, and some don't, although that group is much smaller. Most people are basically nice… and helpful… in varying degrees, and the way forward is to become nicer and more helpful, if you want to put it that way… Onwards and Upwards!"

"I can see that I have lot to learn".

"Everyone has a lot to learn, don't worry about it. It is not a race, but most souls who arrive here need to be reminded about how life works, because the ways of the Surface have become imprinted upon them, but the impression does wear off, if you will allow it to, believe me…"

"It is going to take a bit of getting used to… I can see that… or does that mean that I am making problems for myself?"

"That is up to you. There's nothing wrong with being aware of a situation, but dwelling on it, or worrying about it can make it worse, or even probably will make it worse. There is no need to be paranoid about what you think, but it is definitely worth knowing that what you think exists and could affect you and your existence… even be it only temporarily…"

"The problem here is that in infinity, 'temporarily' could be a very long time… perhaps, thousands of years!"

"Yes, but that needn't be a problem… In infinity, thousands of years is less than a drop in the ocean, since there is a finite number of drops of water on any planet. What I am saying is that nothing can affect you adversely for ever except knowledge and that will always help, even though you, or one, may need to relearn, or remember, some lessons. Nothing can stop the steady improvement of the Self, even if some learn more quickly than others… As I said before, life is not a race or even a competition. And that is something that too many people have to learn, but there Ego's are so fragile that they have to feel superior to those around them.

"The true name of the game, to use an expression, is co-operation, not competition… Life is a team sport, if you like, not a solo event… Treating life like a solo event leads to loneliness, misery and selfishness, whereas if you treat it as a team event, it becomes a party! Or at least can do - that should be the goal".

"You make it all sound so lovely, my darling, Sarah, but then you always did have that knack. There isn't a bad bone in your body…"

She looked herself up and down and smiled, "There aren't any!"

"No, not now, but you know what I mean".

"Yes, thank you, Willy. You're not so bad yourself. You were a good husband and in difficult circumstances. I think we did our best for one another and our daughter".

"Whether it was our doing or hers, or a bit of both, Becky has turned out all right. Anyway, enough of this Mutual Admiration Society meeting, I call it to a close. I'm not used to praise, I can't take it".

"No, I know what you mean… Getting a compliment out of a Welshman is like pulling teeth with chopsticks!"

"Was I that inattentive, Sarah dear? I didn't mean to be… another regret to add to the list…"

"It wasn't only you. It's just the way people were. We were all to busy getting on with a hard life. Don't worry about it, Willy, I know that I nagged you too sometimes".

"Not much, and I probably deserved it. At least I got to get out, and even go to the pub, but that cottage became your jail... and I knew it, but pretended that I didn't, because it suited me - I was selfish and I am so sorry for that now".

"Don't worry about it, Willy. It's all behind us now. You wouldn't be able to do that to me now though, even if you wanted to, although that doesn't mean that I wouldn't let it happen to me again in another incarnation. Life's funny like that".

"If you say so, my dear. Shall we move on now?"

"Sure, if you're ready. Where do you want to go?"

"I don't know... Home, I suppose".

"Home... All right. Do you want to live in town or on the mountain again?"

"Don't you already have somewhere you stay?"

"Er, well, er, it's difficult to explain..." She saw Willy's face reflect an inner turmoil and she guessed what the cause was. "No, it's not that. I haven't shacked up with anyone else - there are no nasty surprises in store for you! It's just that we don't need houses, just like we don't need bodies.

"Think about it. Why do people live in houses?"

"Well, er, it's normal, isn't it?"

"Yes, but they want shelter, privacy and security. However, we don't need to shelter from the weather because we have nothing to shelter and the weather is of our own making. We don't need privacy because we have no bodies, and anyway, if someone saw that you wanted to be alone, they would leave you alone - or most would... And security? We don't have anything that can be stolen..."

"Yes, I see".

"Having said that, lots of people still like to live in something somewhere. Life on the Surface seems to ingrain that very deeply into most people. So, what is it to be, within or without the city walls?"

"The city we were in before?"

"The City of Annwn? Yes, if you like".

"Won't it be hard to find somewhere at such short notice?"

"No, we'll just make the city a bit bigger, and put our house in there; or make a tower a bit taller and put our flat in or on it. Whatever you like. Or we could stay at the Inn while we think about it".

"Yes! I like that idea. We never did get much waiting on, did we? We only ever stayed in a hotel that week on our honeymoon in Rhyl. Yet when we first got married, I did so much want to give you a lady's life of luxury, Sarah. It just didn't work out like that… I'm sorry, my dear, so sorry". Tears flowed down his cheeks. Sarah shuffled over and put her arms around him.

"I know that now, and I knew that then. I knew what I was letting myself in for, and I did it willingly, because I loved, and still love you. You were always the dreamer, not me, Will Jones!"

"You were my rock, Sarah".

"And you mine"

"Come on, let's go and see if there's any room at the Inn".

Willy drew his head back to get a better look at his wife, "Now you're taking the Mick, aren't you?"

"Yes".

"Because there will be, won't there?"

"Yes. You're starting to get the hang of it".

"Will our old drinking mates be there?"

"They could be…"

"… if we want them to be".

"Yes", she said mounting up. "Come on then, Willy boy, race you again, see if you can win this time" and she sped off with the hounds all around her.

"Wait for me! That's not fair! I don't know where Annwn City is! I can't win!" He watched Sarah turn to face him. She was laughing out loud, looked in her twenties and was dressed like a maiden of the Fifteenth Century. He couldn't quite remember, but he was almost certain that she had been wearing her normal Twentieth Century gear a few moments before.

Life in Annwn

They rode and laughed for miles, or was it minutes? Willy could not be certain. It seemed that every time he tried to get a fix on time or a place, it moved. He was trying so hard to think in a linear pattern, but he couldn't. Every time he thought he had a fix on a concept, it seemed to squidge out between his grasp like jelly in a tight fist.

When he looked up from his contemplations, Sarah was rounding behind an outcrop of one of the two mountains and a fear of being alone in this strange land gripped him. He urged his horse on, and found himself at his wife's side. She had stopped to wait for him out of site, but before her was the huge, pinkish, front stone wall of Annwn City.

A flag, a pennant really, Willy thought, fluttered in the breeze atop a round tower within the walls.

"Wow! It's even more beautiful than I remember it", he murmured.

"Good", replied Sarah.

"I don't remember it being pink though".

"Don't you? Oh, well, we can change that…"

"No, I like it… it makes it look more like a comic book castle… no disrespect. More like Camelot in the cartoons, than Camelot…"

"Was there a Camelot?"

"I don't know, but if there were, I should imagine that it would have been more like Caerphilly Castle than that. I like it though, let's go in. Now I can race you to the gates!"

Willy arrived at the moat a length ahead of Sarah, but he knew in his mind that she had let him win. He looked up to the crenellated battlements above the drawbridge to see three men, who he supposed were guards, peering down at him. He turned rather sheepishly to Sarah.

"Guard! Squire William Jones and his wife, Sarah Jones, request entrance to the City of Annwn".

"Good day to you! Why do you make such a request unannounced?"

"We have travelled far and require shelter for a few days".

One guard disappeared, leaving the other two staring at the new arrivals. A minute later, the third man returned. "Your request for shelter has been granted. Please wait while we provide access" and with that chains could be heard clanking, which caused Willy's horse to rear up, and the drawbridge began to drop. When it was halfway down, they could see the portcullis being raised too. Willy grinned at Sarah, as if he were enjoying a role in a film.

When it was down, they trotted over the drawbridge and acknowledged the salutes from the guards inside. 'This way, my Lord", said Sarah light-heartedly and moved up in front. As they reined in their horses outside the inn they had visited before, the same landlord came running out to greet them.

"It is lovely to see you again, my Lord and Lady! I have the finest room anywhere in the city, if that is your requirement. Permit my lad to see to your horses. Boy! The horses, and look sharp about it!"

Willy and Sarah dismounted and followed the landlord inside. "It has been a lovely day, landlord", said Willy getting into the swing of things.

"That it has, my Lord. Indeed it has. Shall I have your things taken up to our finest room?"

Will looked to Sarah, unaware that they had any 'things' to take up.

"Yes, landlord. Please do that, but ask your boy to be careful with them. The caskets hold great sentimental value for us. They have been in my husband's family for generations". Willy looked at Sarah with an open mouth.

""Certainly, milady. Please, take a seat, if that be hour pleasure. Oi! You lot! Keep the noise down or I'll stop your beer! We've got a real gentleman and his lady here now, and they don't want to have to listen to you rabble swearing!"

Willy looked behind him and noticed six men drinking at a table, who he presumed were the same ones as before. Sarah, only smiled at him and urged him by gesture to sit opposite her. "Do you want anything, dear?" she asked.

"I could murder a Ploughman's Lunch and a pint of bitter", he replied. "All that riding had made me right hungry and thirsty". Sarah peered briefly into his eyes, but it was enough to get her message across. She placed the order with their host.

"The riding didn't really make me hungry or thirsty, did it?"

"No", she smiled, "you did. You expected to feel hungry and thirsty… either that or it was he excuse that you might use because you wanted a pint and something to eat. Either way,it doesn't matter".

"Well, what was all that about our luggage? And what 'things'?"

"Oh, that? I was just indulging him, like I do with you. He was expecting us to have luggage, so I decided not to disappoint him. I didn't have to, but, well,it makes him feel better… in the same way that eating and drinking will make you feel better.

"Or to be more accurate, it won't… it will produce the empty satisfaction that buying something gives you. It lasts a few hours or a few days, but then you have to do it again. Like getting drunk every night… sooner or later, it is hoped, one will discover the complete futility of it and fix the cause for wanting to get drunk every night, so that you one can get on with one's real life".

"Which is?"

"Which is to learn, to acquire knowledge, and to put that knowledge to good use by helping others. Wisdom and altruism, in two concepts, if you like. If you have no knowledge, your desire to be helpful or altruistic might actually be harmful. You might do more harm than good… AND by doing good, you enhance your own Karma, thereby helping yourself!"

"Win win", he said, already convinced, but not wanting to hear the old mantra again. Hearing it still made him feel uncomfortable somewhere deep inside, even though he 'knew' it to be true. "Yes, I agree with you, but it doesn't trip off my tongue as easily as it does yours. I'm not ready to sound like a Hari Kishna yet".

"I know you're not, but you have already jumped the highest hurdles. You believe in it, and you live by it - more or less - but you are not yet prepared to come out and admit it to anyone but me".

He looked at her across the table, pursed his lips, then realised that he had done it, and so looked down at his hands. She had always been able to read him like a book, even before she had passed on. He was grateful when the landlady approached them with his food and drink. "Do you want anything, my dear?" he asked, immediately feeling foolish again.

Sarah grinned. "Yes, OK, I'll have a cheese sandwich and a glass of water to keep you company. Thank you". The landlady, a large jovial-looking fifty-odd-year-old in a rough dress and white apron, performed a slight curtsey, smiled broadly, and turned on her heel. "Won't be a jiffy, madam". She returned almost instantaneously and placed her wares before Sarah. "Enjoy your meal. Just shout if you need me. I'll be just behind that wall in the kitchen".

"You didn't have to do that just to please me, Sarah, but that you anyway. The strange thing is that I'm not really hungry any longer".

"That's not all that strange really. What would be strange is if you didn't want that pint either", she replied with a wicked grin.

"Oh, I can still find room for that", he laughed, playing along, but he realised that actually, he could take that or leave it as well. He took a mouthful and licked his lips. "Mmmm, Nectar".

"Get away with you!" Willy looked down again, avoiding her gaze, and was surprised to see that Sarah's plate was empty bar a few crumbs. He looked up to see her watching him and smiled, she tilted her head to the side and smiled back. Everyone was happy - they had all gotten what they wanted. Willy took a bite of cheese and willed he rest away, but he was still surprised when it vanished before his very eyes.

Sarah clapped silently and mouthed 'well done'.

"OK, if we're not going to eat,and not going to drink… very much, what are we going to do? Do you want to go upstairs?"

"Willy Jones! What are you suggesting?" she said pretending to be affronted/offended.

"No, no! I didn't mean it like tha…", but he saw her laughing. "I suppose we are still married, aren't we? Do people, er… does that sort of thing go on here?"

"Yes, it still 'goes on', but we don't have any bodies and don't need to procreate. The thing is that not everyone realises that, so they carry on like they would have on the Surface. It's the same as drinking and eating. If you want to feel close to someone, there are other ways of doing it, which would have happened if you were making love to someone you loved on the Surface.

"We can talk about it again, if you like, but basically, it's more a melding or touching of souls rather than bodies… It's akin to the feeling you get when you meet someone and you like them immediately, or not, as the case may be. That feeling is produced by your non-physical bodies touching and being either in or out of harmony".

"Something else has been bothering me…" Sarah gave a slight upwards nod of encouragement. "Well, let's say that this was an inn with ten bedrooms, and it was full. Then you come along and turn it into an eleven-bedroomed inn, wouldn't the landlord notice? Or are they complicit?"

"No, not complicit, but he or and his wife might be aware of the change, although that is very seldom the case".

"Well, I don't get it then".

"No, it is difficult, but it has to do with parallel existences, worlds or Universes, whatever you want to call them. Here and now, this inn has always had eleven bedrooms, but in another existence, it, or one very much like it, may only have five. If this landlord woke up in the 'morning' and his hotel only had five rooms, he would probably think that he had gone mad.

"Having said that, there are people, or Souls, who know about parallel existences and can move freely between them, because they understand The Truth, and so are not locked in by their own beliefs. It's like the story about elephants…"

"Remind me…"

"Well, a mahout tethers a baby elephant to a deep stake so that it cannot escape. The baby elephant learns that trying to flee is futile and so stops trying. However, later, the elephant weighs two tons and could easily pull up that stake, but he doesn't try to, because he 'already knows' - he has already learned - that it is impossible.

"People do not believe in parallel existences, they are not taught about them on the Surface, or not widely, and so they cannot perceive them.

"If we left this, let's call it, eleven-bedroomed existence without paying our bill, this landlord would remember us for that, but the 'same' landlord in the five-bedroom existence would not know anything about it… or might know, or might have a vague feeling of 'irrational' distrust towards us. It is very difficult to tell how much people know without interacting with them.

"At least,it is for me. Someone more advanced than I might well be able to tell someone's level of attainment from their Aura. I am still learning about these things in school - for want of a better word".

"Yes, I see, said the blind man'. It's a lot to take in, isn't it?"

"Yes, it is, but that is the least of your worries… You, and everybody else, have all the time in the world to work it out. Come on, let's go to our room, and I'll show you what I meant by melding".

Life in Annwn

2. A STITCH IN TIME

Willy opened his eyes cautiously and squinted at the ceiling. He was lying on a bed, presumably in his hotel room, so he looked to his left with a little more confidence to see Sarah lying beside him propped up on her arm smiling at him.

"Good morning, my dear. Did you sleep well?" he asked.

"Yes, you could call it that. Did you?"

"What do you mean by 'You could call it that?' Don't we sleep any more?"

"Did you sleep?"

"Yes, I think I did... didn't I?"

After a fashion. We don't have bodies that require sleep, but our minds benefit from rest, but they don't switch off. Sleeping here is more like meditation, but your mind might not know that yet, so you may still think that you need sleep. That's why I asked you whether you thought that you had slept".

"Well, it felt... I feel as if I did, but if I didn't, what did I do?"

"Did you dream?"

"I don't remember... should I have?"

"You will do one day, but then, one day, you will not find the need to sleep as we knew it. The transition period is similar for most people, but not exactly the same. It's interesting for me to observe how you cope with the transition. I mean, I have studied it at school, but I am not yet working on that area of the condition of the recently deceased".

"You make me sound like a specimen - a lab rat".

"Yes, I know... Sorry about that, but I didn't think that you'd mind".

"I don't really. I'm lucky to have a teacher that I know so well to help me".

"Thank you, but there is always someone to help everyone. If it hadn't been me, it would have been someone else you knew, had met or had heard of".

"So what did we do last night?"

"Not very good for a lady's ego, are you?"

"Sorry, I didn't mean… I mean, I didn't mean that… I meant… Oh, God! I don't know what I meant now!"

"Don't worry, Willy boy, I'm only joking with you! I think that you had a lot of processing to do, so we found somewhere quiet, and you shut down, went into meditation, if you like, to make sense of all the things that you have experienced recently. That's all, and I stayed to watch over you, in case you had any questions, which you didn't.

"You have lived here before - everyone has - but after a time on the Surface, we forget most of what we knew about here… or, at least, most people do. Some are born on the Surface and it all comes back to them. Then, when you return here, your mind has to set aside some of the functions it had on the Surface and relearn The Truth - Reality.

"As I said, some people cling to their Surface life for a lot longer than others, some adapt more quickly".

"What about me?"

"I think that you will adapt quickly, Willy. You are not a doubter, you are a believer, and a searcher after The Truth. I can see it in your Aura, but I have known it for a long time. I have been with you every step of the way since I got here… I have never left your side".

"I knew you wouldn't leave me… and I could feel you there sometimes. You were a great comfort to me… You and old…"

"Kiddy! Me and old Kiddy - the dog! You haven't lost your old charm have you!"

"I didn't mean it like that…"

"Yes you did, but I am not upset. Why would I be? Never lie to cover up your feelings… it doesn't work here. Would you like to see her?"

"Can I?"

"Of course, you can. Call her".

No sooner had he called her name than she jumped up onto the bed, rubbed along his side and licked his face.

"Hello, girl. It's lovely to see you again". Her tail was wagging, she was panting and her eyes were shining. Willy ruffled the hair on her head. "Life couldn't get much better than this!" he exclaimed beaming. "Although bacon, sausage and eggs wouldn't go amiss…"

Sarah, shook her head slowly, but got off the bed. "I'll ask the landlady to send up breakfast on a tray".

∞

After he had eaten and given the scraps to his dog, Willy stretched out on the bed again. "I might jot have needed that, but it sure tasted great, and it felt good to share the bacon rind with Kiddy too".

"Don't worry about it, it's not hurting anyone".

"So, my dear, what are we going to do today?" he asked from his prone position, his hands behind his head and Kitty by his side. Sarah tilted her head at him as a teacher might a child who got a times table wrong. "Now, I mean, not today".

"We can do anything you want, but if you are leaving it up to me, we could take a closer look at time and other existences. Would that suit his Lordship?"

"Yes, it would My Lady, it sounds very interesting indeed".

"OK, whenever you're ready".

"Don't I need a shower first? No, I don't suppose I've got anything to wash, have I?"

Sarah grinned and shook her head again. "No… How is your memory of British battles or recent wars like the Second World War?"

"I never did like history. It was always King so-and-so did this, or Queen so-and-so did that… All lies and propaganda, if you ask me. I was a kid during the Second World War though, and vaguely remember that. Why?"

"You'll see. I want to tell you a little about my work first though".

"I have a vague memory of you mentioning that before, but my memories of Annwn were all rather hazy, like dreams, once I'd woken up".

"Yes, that's normal for someone without training. Anyway, one of the most common jobs here - although it's not really a job - is to go out looking for 'lost' or confused Souls. You must have heard people say that people, er, dead people… friends and family, who have already passed over, come to help you over at the moment of your passing. Well, that is true, but sometimes, we are unable to get there in time. Like at a mass killing or huge natural disaster.

"It can happen to individuals too - ones who are really set in their beliefs. Catholics are a good example, or they were. These days, many Catholics have had their faith undermined, but it's not only the fanatically religious. Remember I told you about Henry VIII still strutting around ordering people about? Well, we've quite a few of those too.

"Anyway, we have… er, counsellors, you might call them, who seek out such people and try to put them straight. It's one of the first jobs when one starts a life dedicated to helping others".

"It sounds pretty important to me…"

"Yes, it is, but it is humbling to see the state of misery that some poor Souls have gotten themselves into. The first job is actually comforting abused animals… that's pretty tough too. The things some of us do to them… it's heart-breaking". For the first time in several decades, Willy thought that he saw tears in her eyes, but he didn't like to mention it.

"So, if you're ready, we'll look at both of these concepts, as the one is very much related to the other". She lay down bedside him on the bed. "Give me your hand. Now, I have no warn you that this might be shocking, and even frightening, even very frightening. We don't have to hold hands throughout, but whatever you do, stay by my side. Don't go wandering off! And there is no need to take shelter - there is nothing there that can hurt us. Don't forget that… we don't have bodies, so nothing there can hurt us in the slightest. OK? Right. Just follow my lead, and just watch".

A moment later, they were standing in a sodden field, but neither of them was heavy enough to sink into the mud. It was drizzling slightly.

"Why have we come here - wherever here is?"

"Here is Agincourt. Remember the famous battle? Longbows and all that?". William nodded, while looking around him. "That will take place here in three days time". Willy stopped, let go of her hand and stared at her, doubt written all over his face. "Oh yes, it is October 22nd, 1415. The French will come from that side and the British from over there. Watch… it is the 25th… now!"

Instantly, there were dead and dying men all around them and arrows were falling from the sky like rain. Men were screaming in pain with horrific injuries. "Help me, sister, please! I beseech you, for the love of God, please help me!". The French soldier raised an arm towards Sarah, but was pierced by two more arrows as he spoke and died instantly.

"He, he, he could see you!" stammered Willy, covering his head with his hands.

"Yes. You know that some people can and others cannot. It has always been thus. Take your hands down, Willy! These shafts weigh two to three ounces or even more. They are penetrating armour! Your hands are no protection. At the height of this short first phase of the battle about a thousand of these thirty-inch arrows were being fired every second. Between five and six thousand Frenchmen and four hundred Brits will die today, and many of them won't even know what hit them.

"The lucky ones will know immediately that they have passed over, others will need a little persuasion from people like me, and others will take much longer to be convinced. Look, our Guides are already arriving". She pointed at people walking among the dead and dying impervious to the lethal missiles.

"And here we are today, in the same spot. Look over there! A Frenchman is sitting with his back to a tree, an arrow sticking vertically out of his shoulder. There has to be two foot of arrow buried in that man, probably killing him instantly, but he refuses to believe it. He is waiting for someone to rescue him. You will find others around here too, still hiding from the British camp followers who would have cut their throats after the battle and robbed them.

"Come, let's go".

"Yes, please. This is dreadful... the suffering is palpable. Where next?"

They were standing in a dusty wasteland. There were small fires consuming what little combustible material that was left. A few low cornice walls jutted up in the otherwise complete flatness; dust-devils whirled across the ground and wisps of smoke rose into the air. They took a few paces forward, and Sarah pointed to a black man huddled against the two-foot high remnants of a heavy stone wall. He was hugging his knees, his bald head down, and he was crying.

"Fat Man struck here three hours ago", said Sarah, "but this man still doesn't acknowledge that. He saw his daughter disappear in front of him. She was only a yard in front of him, but just around the corner. She took a direct hit from the blast and was vaporized, but this man, her father took longer to die from his burns He won't believe that though.

"We call him Otokoshtori - it means, 'I am all alone' in Japanese. It is all he has said since August 9th, 1945. This is Hiroshima. 150,000 died here as a result of one bomb - about half on the first day, and there are tens of thousands like poor Otoshtori wandering around here - selfish though he is to be worried only about his own predicament. Perhaps that's why he can't move on".

"I'm sure you recognize this, eh?"

"I sure do! Good old Cardiff Castle! I suppose that must have seen some battles too, dating from the Roman times".

"Yes, it's seen its share all right, but that's not what I want to show you. Look over here. See him?"

"Yes, a tramp, not too old either, sleeping in the bushes".

"Yes, but he wasn't a tramp. Do you remember the German raid in January 1941, when a parachute mine landed on The Hollyman Bakery in Grangetown killing thirty-two people?"

"Vaguely", he shrugged, "but not really".

"Well, Ifor, here's, family were in that basement, or some of them were anyway. So, the next time he was back on leave from the continent, he went AWOL and hitched back here, although he walked most of the way to avoid the police and so on. It was late April, 1941 when he arrived... the 29th, in fact. It was already quite late, so he decided to go for a few beers and sleep in the Castle Gardens before searching for his family the following morning.

"There was another raid that night, about thirty-three people were killed on Riverside that night, and the papers reported that one parachute mine fell 'harmlessly into the Castle Grounds'. Except that it wasn't so harmlessly... It fell on Ifor while he was out cold. He still doesn't know that it happened, or won't believe it. Every day, he goes looking for his family, and every night he come back here to sleep, because to him, every day is April 30th.

"The pity of it all, besides his misconception, is that the army and his family believed that he was a deserter and a coward, but luckily he doesn't know that either.

"Come on, let's go back to Annwn. You look worn out and bubbling with questions".

Willy propped himself up on his elbow and faced his wife. "Was that a dream?" he asked.

"No, my dear. It was as real as anything that has ever happened to you".

"I suppose there was Aberfan too?"

"Yes..."

"It was awful... but you said that I looked worn out".

"Yes, in the sense of emotionally drained, not physically tired. And there are millions of sites like that all over this planet, and billions of them all over the Universe. It's a joke to think that all we do is sit on a cloud playing a harp, or walk in the Garden of Eden sniffing flowers... and that is just one of the tasks we perform, although it is true to say that not everybody helps out".

"So, what is it that you do?"

"Well, as you saw, we can revisit those parallel existences any time we like, so, we visit these sites regularly and keep on trying to prove that they are dead, but not dead and gone, if you see what I mean. The day after the Battle of Agincourt took place, for example, there were hundreds who needed our help, but now, there there are only a few dozen. We keep chipping away, reducing the numbers… The same with every war zone, natural disaster or plane crash".

"Wow, is the only word that comes to mind. But tell me, what would happen if you didn't do this work… I mean, if no-one did it?"

"Oh, they would realise The Truth in time, but, despite infinity, we try to speed up the process in order to relieve suffering".

"Yes, I can see that. Is that where Catholics get the idea of Purgatory from? Do you think I'd be able to do this sort of work too?"

"I don't know about Purgatory, but it could be. It is possible that it is a description of this state that has become blurred over time by people who didn't quite understand the predicament… but yes, Willy, I do think you could do this work. It only takes compassion, and I know that you have that in abundance. I can get you on a course whenever you think you're ready".

"I'd really like to help, but I'm just worried whether I could cope after seeing what I did earlier. Far from being the easiest job, it seems to me that they are throwing novices in at the deep end!"

"No, jot really. First, there is no 'they'. Nobody forces anyone to do anything they don't want to or feel up to. Then there are no set hours. People do what they feel they are capable of… that's all. Because of the nature of time here, there are no days, no nine-to-five jobs. When you feel charged enough, you might like to help. That's all… and yes, it is a stressful job, but it is not the only thing that needs doing.

"There is also the matter of abused animals, but that is not always less stressful. Don't feel obliged to help… it is not incumbent upon anyone. Having said that tough, I know you, and you will want to help, and so, you will find a way to do that. Don't worry about it now".

"Perhaps, I could start with local disasters…?"

She smiled, "There is no reason why you can't have a special interest, but nationalities don't make much difference here. We have visitors from all over the Galaxy, indeed, all over the Universe and other parallel existences…"

"No, it's not that I only want to help Welsh people, but Aberfan, coal mine disasters and perhaps local battles, might be a better place for me to start".

Sarah patted his hand. "Whatever you say, Willy, whatever you say, but you might want to rethink that one day, but that is completely up to you. Why don't you try to get some rest now, my dear? I'll still he here when you're ready". Willy offered up a kiss, and then closed his eyes like a good child being put to bed.

"I am a bit tired… I mean emotionally drained", he muttered and went off somewhere in his head to recharge his batteries.

Life in Annwn

3 PICKING UP A PREVIOUS LIFE

"OK, my dear, do you feel better now? It was a harrowing experience, wasn't it? Perhaps, I shouldn't have been so brutal, but I judged that, since our generation missed actually taking part in any battles, since we have never witnessed the horrors of warfare, that it might be better to show you what really goes on. Please forgive me if I got it wrong".

"No, it's alright, Sarah, but, it was a Hell of shock... er, if I can use that expression".

"Oh, yes, that isn't a problem!" she laughed. "They are one and the same place. The two extremes... the two faces of the same coin, but with, most people say, five gradations in between them... the Seven Heavens, you've heard of".

"Yes, I understand, so what level are we on?"

"It's not always easy to tell. It's not like seven floors in an hotel... it's more imaginary than that... a feeling, a vibration. The higher the level, or Plane, the higher the vibration, and the more Spiritual, and consequently, less physical.

"Not only that, but people are not confined to one level. Like in school. Er, we are more like bubbles in a Space Lamp... we can rise to a higher plane by employing correct though, or sink by being base, mean or nasty. You could say that we drift between the Planes depending on who we are talking to, and what we are talking or thinking about.

"The point is that everybody feels happiest at a certain level, or on a certain Plane, and so they will tend to gravitate back to that Plane, even though they may have been on a higher or lower one temporarily. A good example is a typical Sunday back home on our mountain.

"On Sunday morning, you get ready for Chapel. You have a wash, put your best clothes on and walk down to the Church, where you listen to an uplifting sermon, sing a few hymns, and feel good about yourself. You might even make a promise to yourself to become a better person from then on. Then you go to the pub, get drunk with your mates, play cards, start swearing and blaspheming, and accuse Tommy Atkins of cheating again!"

"He does cheat when he's drunk!"

"Well, maybe he does, but that's not the point I was making, is it? Or perhaps it is... Old Tommy would have been in Chapel too, but it didn't change him for long".

"No, I understand..."

"Anyway, shall we go out and see if we can find something interesting for you to do?"

"Sure! It would be nice to have a look around the city again... not that I remember much about it from the last time. It was like a dream. The more I think about the physical details, and try to pin them down - to remember them - the harder it gets, yet I think I remember what we talked about".

"That's pretty typical too. It's because there were no buildings, and there are no buildings. They are just a figment of our, or especially your imagination, because you cannot conceive of a city without them, script you mind fills in the blanks. The really important stuff, the words, the conversation and the ideas, it does remember more easily, because that is all there really was.

"We exchanged ideas, but for you to feel comfortable... at ease, that had to be done in chairs, and chairs are in buildings, and buildings are in cities, although it doesn't really matter what form those chairs or buildings take. Hence, they are unimportant - immaterial - to the dialogue, which was the important part.

"Does that make sense, dear?"

"Yes, what we talked about was important and real, so I remembered it, but the settings in which the conversation took place were imaginary, so I didn't".

"Yes... you always were better with words than me. So, shall we go?"

"I'm ready, but I am supposing that that means that the city might not be exactly the same as last time, right?"

"Right. It will be as similar to last time as I remember it, but since you don't remember it perfectly either, it doesn't matter, does it?"

"No!" he laughed and followed her out of their room, down the stairs and onto the street.

There were children chasing geese on the cobblestone square outside, and that was surrounded by market stalls behind which traders were hawking their wares of fruit, meat, vegetables, and clothing.

"So, this is all a product of your imagination?" he said to Sarah, as she slipped her arm through his reminding him of old times on their mountain.

"Yes, although I think you are adding bits as well. Some of the details are not mine and this is our illusion - what we call Maya here after the Hindu and Buddhist traditions. A goose caused Willy to come to an abrupt halt to avoid tripping over it as it squawked past inches in front of him.

"You did that on purpose, didn't you?". Sarah nodded and smiled.

"Yes, sorry. I couldn't resist it!"

"I'll get you back for that later!" He raised her hand to his lips and kissed it. "Oh, Sarah, Sarah, Sarah! My beautiful, Sarah! You cannot believe how much I have missed you since… er, you came here, and I could no longer see or hear you clearly…" She saw tears in his eyes and dabbed at them with a dainty silk handkerchief.

"I know, but we're all right now… we're together again. Look, do you remember the tower with the foot baths? Was it round or square?"

"Round, I think. I seem to remember it being like a lighthouse".

"OK, round it shall be. Let's go in. It is one of our schools".

"Yes, I remember. Do want me to go through the Akashic Record again?"

"No, you do what you please. Your progress is no-one's business but your own… It's not even mine, no matter how much I love you. If you ever feel the need to atone for something that is nagging away at the back of your mind, you can come here at any time and check it out".

"Well, what are we going to do here?"

"Nothing specific. Just walk to the top of the tower, look out over the land and then walk back down again. Is that all right with you?"

"Yes, whatever you like, my dear?"

They walked up the stone spiral staircase past scores of heavy, mitre-shaped timber doors, most of which were slightly ajar. Willy often touched the huge stone blocks that made up the walls to test them, but they felt real enough to him. After a while of climbing, the reached a final door. Sarah turned the large, black metal ring which was the handle and pushed the solid door open.

"No, after you, my dear", he said quite seriously, but then added as a joke, "I don't want to step out of the door and fall thirty floors into the moat... Your sense of humour has changed, my girl".

She slapped his shoulder as she passed by, and he slapped her bottom. She made an exaggerated move forward. "Hey! Less of that!" she complained not meaning it. "What do you think of the view? Isn't it marvellous?"

"It sure is. So our mountain is er, over there?"

"If you like".

"Well, the sun... Oh, there is no sun". Sarah was shaking her head. "And no scenery? And no tower?"

"Well... they do exist, but they are certainly not as solid as you perceive them. To you the atoms look dense and solid, whereas, in reality, they are far enough apart to be able to walk through. Look". Sarah stepped through the battlement and stood in 'empty space'. "Come on out and try it. You can't fall - there's nowhere to fall from or to and even if a pedant says that there is, we don't have enough mass to hurt ourselves, and even if we could hurt ourselves, we would be able to fix ourselves immediately". Sarah held out her hand to him and Willy and Willy put his best foot forward towards it.

"That's amazing!" he said taking her hand and smiling back at her. "Truly, bloody amazing!"

"Willy! I didn't like swearing before and I still don't like it now! Speak how you like when you are alone or with your mates, but not when you are with me, please!"

"Yes, sorry, love, but you've got to admit that it's not every day that you find out that you can fly… and walk on water too, I suppose?"

"Sure, but what water?"

"So, that's how He did it? It was just a trick in front of the ignorant savages!?"

"Well, I wouldn't have expressed it quite lime that. The Jews of that period were about as educated as any other people, but they were ignorant of the true facts of life, yes. Just as most people still are now, two thousand years later. And I wouldn't call it a trick… are striking a match or shooting a bird out of a tree tricks? Just because someone has never seen it done before, doesn't make it a trick! Jesus isn't a con man…"

"No, you're right… Sorry, I didn't mean to imply that he was… er, is. Sorry, Jesus".

"Don't worry about it. Let's go back to the tower and take a seat".

"A seat? But I didn't see any sea… Oh, those seats? Silly me". Willy dusted off the stone slab bench and they sat, with their arms on the wall looking out at the scenery that Sarah had created for their enjoyment, just as an artist might create a painting for the delectation of art lovers.

"So, you think that disaster rescue might be too much for you?"

"Yes, well, certainly at the moment. I never did like injury and sickness. I would have made a rotten nurse".

"OK, how about comforting mistreated animals and lonely or neglected children? Or being with people who are dying alone? Not those necessarily in distress, but those who are alone at the point of passing over?"

"I thought friends and family did that?"

"Well, they do normally. If they care enough, but there are still people who die alone, or would do, if it were not for volunteers on this side. In fact, it is becoming an increasingly bigger problem, especially in the West, but all over the world. People are becoming more individual, more independent, and a consequence of that is that they often die alone too.

"However, it is not only those cases. There are also drownings, suicides and routine accident victims… even if they don't end up dying. They often appreciate someone to talk to until physical help arrives. You may even talk someone out of committing suicide. That's a nice feeling".

"Yes. I'm pretty certain that I could do any of those jobs, although watching animals suffer would be tough".

"Yes, it is. Harder than working on the battlefields. For me, anyway, but I did it for a while, and still would if necessary".

"You always were a selfless, hard-working woman, Sarah, and I am ashamed to say that I took advantage of that sometimes".

She took his hand. "Not too often, or I would have left… but I have always loved you, Willy, and knew that you weren't the big tough man you pretended to be".

He choked back a splutter, and turned to wipe his eyes. She knew him well, he thought, but said, "So, up here, we don't have to to eat, drink, sleep or er, procreate, but it seems that we still have to keep busy. That's the one thing I have discovered that we have in common with people in our mortal phase".

"Yes, I suppose you're right. The activities you mentioned are really only necessary for the body, which we 'up here', by which I assume you mean on this tower, no longer have. However, keeping busy has to do with the mind, which we in Annwn do still have. On the other hand, we have our hermits too, although there aren't many, and they are usually old men who were hermits on Earth and can't imagine a different existence. I know that hermits have the reputation for being highly Spiritual, but not all of them made it that far and they are still trying to here in Annwn. A bit like old Henry VIII, the poor man".

"You are a better person than I am, Sarah. I've got no sympathy for the rich bast… er, privileged old sod. I've got no time for kings and queens lording it over everyone… even if he was, is, was a Welsh monarch. He and his ilk don't care about people like us when they are in power, so why should we care about them when they are making complete tits, er, I mean, arses, er fools of themselves."

"It's called compassion and forgiveness, my dear. They behaved foolishly when they had the chance to be great leaders who benefited their people, but they chose to be selfish and greedy. They were week, but acted aggressively in order to hide it.

"But they can't escape from their deeds. Karma keeps track of everything that everyone does. Hating Henry won't cause him to suffer any more, and won't do you any good either, whereas trying to help him might help him and your own Karma.

"Vengeance is not yours, it is Karma's! And we are often our own worst critics, when we are faced with our own stupidity".

"Anyway, let's change the subject for now. So, you think that you would like to help lonely and abused children and people are facing death alone, but who not frightened of the prospect?"

"Yes, that's it. I think it would suit me to slip into this role gently. How about hobbies? Do you have them here?"

"Yes. You like gardening, don't you?"

"Yes, but correct me if I'm wrong, but imagining a beautiful back garden full of healthy flowers is a bit facile, isn't it?"

"Yes, indeed it would be, although you and I would derive pleasure from sitting in and looking at it. There's no harm in that, but that is not what we call gardening. That is more like creating… art, if you like. What we call gardening is something quite different.

"The whole Universe is our garden! Let me give you an example. You could pick an endangered species of, say, tropical orchid, and try to ensure that it survives long enough for some caring people to discover and save it. It's not really my line, but perhaps you get my drift. I could put you in touch with people who know more though.

"How does that sound? There are literally billions of species of flora and fauna that are crying out for help across the Galaxies. It's a great excuse for foreign travel too!"

"Do we need an excuse?"

Life in Annwn

"No, of course not, but I tend to get so engrossed in my work that I don't go anywhere, whereas you could choose species that forced you to travel. If that's what you want".

"I think I would rather like to be around you" he said sheepishly.

"Now that does really does deserve a kiss!" she said, planting one briefly on his lips. "Shall we live in here, in the city, or our there?" she asked sweeping the horizon with her hand.

"Well, if we can travel any distance in an instant, and travel to any minute in history and still be on time, I don't suppose that it matters, does it, as long as we're together?"

"I love you, Willy, and I think you are beginning to get the hang of things again. Shall we go back to the inn?"

"Why not? It's as good a place as any".

4 FINDING A JOB

William 'woke up' on the bed in their room at the inn again, but Sara was reading a book at a round table in the bay window not far away. He put his hands under his head and watched her, thinking that she wouldn't have noticed him awaking because he could see more of her back than her front. It seemed that she was reading a little and then staring out of the window to think about it.

If he wasn't already enamoured, he would have fallen in love all over again, he thought.

"Are you staring at me, Willy Jones?, she asked turning slowly, finishing a sentence, he presumed.

"Ye, you're beautiful".

"Thank you, I'm sure".

"You know, for a man who can't get tired because he hasn't go a body, I get awfully tired and sleep a lot".

"It is not your body that needs rest. Life in corpore is stressful, and everyone goes through a lot both living on the Surface and transitioning to here. You, your Soul, has a lot of information to process and assimilate. Not only that, but you have to relearn how to live here. Don't worry. It's normal".

"It strikes me, you know, that this is what a man feels like recovering from amnesia, not that I've ever had amnesia… or concussion then. Remember when I tripped over that rock and banged my head twenty-odd years ago?"

"Well, I wasn't there was I? It happened when you were drunk walking back from the pub one Sunday afternoon. When you were late for dinner, I came looking for you, and found you sitting in the grass on the roadside. You had no idea where you were!"

Life in Annwn

"I wasn't drunk, I was concussed..."

"You were absolutely blotto!"

"I was concu..."

"Remember what I said about lying?"

"Well, I was concussed... and blotto. Anyway, what are you reading? I hadn't thought about people reading in Annwn".

"It's a book about loneliness and it's effect on the undeveloped mind".

"Wow! You used to like Mills & Boon!"

"Those days are in a different existence. I always knew that there had to be more to life, but I just didn't have the education, or perhaps, gumption, to find out what else there really was. It's easier here. You will never be told that something you learned in Annwn, was not actually the truth. There is no Thirty-Year Rule constructed to conceal The Truth from people so that the rich and powerful can get away with telling lies until after they have passed away. The Truth here always has been and always will be The Truth - unlike on the Surface.

Class barriers and unequal educational opportunities are non-existent in Annwn. In fact, it often works the other way".

"How do you mean?"

"Well, often, when a rich, well-educated, privileged person comes here, they think that they are still superior - like poor old Henry again - and those preconceptions get in the way of his or her progress. Whereas, when someone like me comes here, we know that we have a lot to learn, and so we just get on with it. However, and this is the massive difference, he we only learn The Truth. The lies and propaganda often preached on the Surface do not exist here.

"Here, all knowledge is good knowledge - none of it will ever hold you back ever. That makes it easy to catch up with the more privileged".

"What did Jesus say? 'It is easier for a poor man to pass through the eye of a needle, than it is for a rich man to enter the Kingdom of Heaven'?"

"Yes, well, that is not quite true, but what was actually said might have become distorted in translation or by someone who didn't understand what he was reading, but yes, the gist of The Truth is there, isn't it?"

"Can I have a look at your book?"

"If you want". She appeared at his side, handed it over smiling and then sat down next to him. He didn't read the cover, as she had expected, but opened it to a random inside page.

He looked, moved the book to and fro to adjust the focus of his eyes, and said, "I didn't think that I would need my specs here, but I can't read the letters".

"No, but it has nothing to do with your eyes. It is written in an off-world language. Xian, we call it here. I have studied Xian, and even been there a few times. We'll go one day, if you like?"

"One day?"

"It's just an expression".

"Yes, I'd love to. I didn't travel very far as a shepherd… nor did you".

"No, and I still don't compared with many people, but there's no rush. Have you thought any more about keeping busy?"

"I don't know whether I have or not to be honest, but I do know that I will have to do something. Not only that, but I suppose you have things to do too".

"Oh, don't worry about me. You are my priority - everyone understands that".

"OK, thanks. As far as having something to do goes, we'll just go with Plan B… not the battlefields, the other one".

"OK, good. Let me know when you're ready".

"Now is as good a time as any. How do you know where a suffering animal, or a lonely child is located?"

"There are two basic approaches. Find out for yourself or get someone to tell you".

"Crikey, I should have been able to work that out for myself! Are you taking the Arthur Bliss?"

"Arth… do you have to be coarse?" she asked decoding the Cockney Rhyming Slang that she hadn't heard for decades. "No, I am not. It might sound obvious, but that's how many things work here. It is a simple method, and it works wonderfully. However, as in many cases here, there is the easy way for the lazy, and the other, more independent method for those who like to learn.

"If you want to be completely independent, you w need to learn how to divine misery. It is not difficult, but most people do need to be taught how to do it. An equivalent is the knack you have of finding a pub in a city you've never been to before. Anyway, until you have mastered that skill, if you want to start immediately, you will have to ask someone, won't you?

"It is that simple".

"OK, sounds logical. Ask whom?"

"Me, for example!"

"OK, so you can do that?"

"Yes, don't look so surprised! Why shouldn't I be able to?"

"No, there's no reason. It's just that your stock of new talents overwhelmed me".

"Well, they're not all new, are they. Rediscovered, perhaps, some of them, and a few new ones learned. It will be the same for you. You've forgotten, that's all".

"OK, remind me how to tune into, say, misery".

"OK, the basics. As we said last time you were here, every sentient being is attached to a grid - like a spider's web or computer memory with every intersection representing a being. So, if you scan that grid looking for the low vibrations that misery produce, you will find miserable beings. Experience will teach you the exact vibrations you are looking for - the ones that represent the type of misery that you are looking for, and some of the other vibrations will indicate what sort of being is producing them - a dog, a cat or a human".

"And that's it?"

"Yes, but it's like anything, eh? You know how to play darts, but you never played for Wales, did you? It is easy to describe, but harder to do well, because that takes lots of practice and a certain amount of dedication. However, once you have learned that skill, there are other uses you can put it to.

"Like most things here, you can use helping others to promote your own skills and abilities, or you can just ask someone to help you. It's up to you".

"I would like to learn, or relearn, the skill to be able to use the grid, or do you call it the web?"

"Either. You will hear both, and other words".

"Where do I enrol? That sounds like the best place to start".

"I can teach you, or we can easily find you someone else, if you like".

"No, I want you to teach me?"

"Good. Lie down again and shift over".

"But I always lie on the right! That's my side…"

"Not this time, it's not!"

∞

"That was wonderful! So, moving… Some people are so thoughtless, aren't they? That poor little puppy! They just left him all alone in the flat, and he only looked about six weeks old".

"Yes, but it's not always thoughtlessness. The parents are probably at work and the kids in school. Maybe they've never had a dog before. Don't rush to judge them, but the puppy was in a terrible state".

"He's just been dragged away from his mum and siblings. He's scared and lonely and in a strange house"

"No food and no water! It's disgraceful. People like that shouldn't be allowed to own an animal… or they should be made to go to night school to learn how to care for them. They should need a certificate before they can buy a dog!"

"Yes, all right, dear. There are thousands of cases like that, and millions of much worse examples".

"Well, it was really gratifying to keep him company. He really appreciated it, didn't he? He's a lovely little chap… not much good as a sheepdog, but a grand pet and guard dog… or will be one day… and yet that's how they treat him! It should be against the law…"

"Yes, all right, love. Don't go on about it, do something about it instead!"

"I will. I'm going back tomorrow, or wherever you tell me he's lonely next. He could see us, couldn't he?"

"Yes, animals and many children can. They haven't been persuaded that we don't exist".

"I'd love to go see him when the family is at home. He'd be playing with us, and the family wouldn't have a clue what was going on! That would be funny… and they would call him, but he wouldn't come, because he knows us better than he does them!"

"Yes, you have to be careful with that, Willy. You don't want him to be punished because you want to gratify your ego. The point is to help the dog, not so that you can prove a point. It can be very fine line… not unlike the one that temporary foster parents have to walk".

Willy took a deep breath and exhaled an even deeper sigh. "I guess you're right, but it would be nice, eh?" Sarah nodded, but flattened her lips. "I enjoyed that, and definitely want to keep doing it - and I want to learn how to locate the animals on my own, although it was great to play with the dog with you too.

"I don't suppose you find endangered plants in the same way, eh? I mean, do plants get lonely or feel threatened when there aren't many of them left? I remember Prince Charles saying that his plants listen to him or something like that, but what goes on there?"

"It's even easier actually".

"What, plants leave an even stronger trace than puppies?"

"No, you just ask the locals", she laughed. "Plants thrive in a happy environment. That is true, so if they cannot be in their natural environment, they grow better in a happy home, but their vibes are too faint for me. No, in that case, it is better to ask the people who live in the area".

"What if they don't believe in, er, us?"

"Peoples in remote places often do believe in Spirit though. It's the city folk who often have the doubts, and luckily, there are not many endangered species in the cities... not compared with in the wild, anyway, but we have another resource that might sound a little over-the-top to you at the moment.

"The Little Folk..."

"Y Tylwyth Teg? Fairies?"

"Yes. I know that you suspected they existed when you were with the sheep on the mountain, but you were right, you did see them, and they know everything that there is to know about flowers... well, all flora and fauna, in fact".

"I knew I had seen them! I blood... sorry, I knew that my eyes weren't playing tricks on me, as sure as eggs is eggs! Whoo-hoo! I knew it! Up with y Tylwyth Teg!

"Do they live here in Annwn too?"

"Er, they live everywhere, but they keep themselves to themselves. They are in a parallel existence, but it is very close to the sight range of human eyes. Animals can see them more easily. You can befriend them, but they don't take to everyone, and don't really encourage contact. Nothing stopping you from trying though".

"And they are shortish, wear green and tend plants?"

"More or less exactly as the stories tell, yes".

"Wow! That's great news! And they don't regard us as competition?"

"No, more of a nuisance, as far as I can tell. I've never actually met any, though I have seen them. They have a few people who they trust, but there aren't many. There's no animosity or anything like that, just a kind of dissonance which keeps us apart... like distant relatives that you think there was a feud with before you were born, but nobody can remember what it was about".

Willy nodded, but was deep in thought. "I'd like to meet them sometime".

"Perhaps you will if you really want to. I'm told that there are other species of man on Earth too, but I have never met any of them either. I have met other species from other planets though, and I am certain that you will meet some of them sometime".

"I can't wait. I used to wonder what there would be to do in Heaven before. I never in my wildest dreams thought that there could be so much".

"And we've only just scratched the surface, my dear. There is no need to be bored in Annwn, I can tell you that for certain".

"Well, I would like to work with endangered plants too, and if I could work with the Fairies, that would be a super bonus".

"OK, there's no harm in hoping and trying. Good luck with it".

Willy could tell from her voice that she did not hold out much hope of him being able to establish any kind of meaningful rapport with the Fair Family that old folk had talked about roaming Wales since time immemorial, but he had heard, via legend and myth that they did talk to some humans, and he wanted to be one of them.

5 GETTING THE BASICS RIGHT

"Come on then, Willy, m'lad, I think it's time we went house-hunting".

"Er, yes, sure. Why not, but if you have been feeling like this, you should have mentioned it before".

"No, it's not that. I'm quite happy here, I've been waiting for you to take a decision. Don't you want us to have our own place?"

"Well, yes, but I am still following your lead".

"Mmm, well, now I want you to take the initiative".

"All right, I will! Let's go and look for somewhere more permanent to live!"

She smiled at him and shook her head slowly. "And when do you want to do this?"

"Er, shall we go now?" Sarah creased her eyes. "Yes, we ought to go now, right this instant!"

"You don't want to check out after breakfast?" she joked, but he took her seriously.

"Yes, I suppose that would make more sense… Hey, wait a minute! I haven't eaten for days, have I? I mean, we don't have to eat any more, do we?"

"Willy, Willy, Willy… my darling Willy… it still hasn't q registered with you has it?"

"No, he", looking forlorn and playing with his hands in his lap. "I can't quite get my head around this new concept of time".

"No, fair enough. It isn't easy, but it is easier to just live it and let it sink in naturally… like learning a new language. It is easier to learn French while living in France, than it is from a book in a classroom".

"Well, I'm not hungry, so that's one thing, I know, but I have no idea when I last ate… I suppose you would say that that is a good thing too".

Sarah nodded.

"Saying that though, I have no idea how long I have been in Annwn. Has it been long?"

"In Surface days? A few weeks. In Annwn time? Nothing at all".

"You see, that's what I'm having trouble with. How can time spent equal nothing?"

"OK. Try to think of it like this. It may help. On the Surface, they measure time using the Sun, but we don't, since there are billions of Suns, and half the time not even one of them figures in our lives. Then, you measure the number of times a planet, sorry, the Earth can go around that Sun in a typical life on the Surface, which is seventy years times three hundred and sixty-five and a quarter days. Then you further sub-divide that. So let's say that the average life is about six hundred thousand hours, but most people do not become aware of this until about a third of them has already gone.

"It means that, on a macro scale, we are always aware that we might be getting too old to have children, or to get a decent education, or to go travelling the world, or to plant crops or to do something perceived as supreme important; and then on a micro scale, we have twenty minutes to get to work, thirty minutes to get to work etc, etc… or in your case, ten minutes before the bar closes.

"All this is because we think that our time is limited. We think of it as a finite resource - 'Time is money!' - and no-one has enough of that, do they?

"Right, and then you come here and time is limitless, infinite. Six hundred thousand hours is meaningless. Yes, OK, if you want to count them by, you can, but when you have reached that magic number, you can do it billions of billions of times over and nothing will have changed. You will be no older and look no different; that bed you're sitting on will not have rotted away, and this inn will not have crumbled into dust, so what is the point?

"If you tried to get all mathematical about it, and said, "OK, we'll have one Surface second equal to a billion years in Annwn', you would still be under-valuing the duration of that second by an immeasurable amount.

"So, yes, in a sense, time does pass here, but only relative to other places. So, our Becky is now a few weeks older, and the flowers cut for your grave have wilted, but you look and behave younger".

"Because I want to...?"

"Yes, if you like, or because that is the frequency that your attitude resonates at... and that vibration produces what you look like. You can change that. You can even shapeshifter, but without a lot of practice, it is difficult to maintain the image for a long time... and by that, I mean relative to someone else".

"Yes, easy when you put it like that, isn't it?" He was being sarcastic, but Sarah ignored it.

"I'm glad that you feel more enlightened".

"Yeah, well, like you say, I'll probably pick it up one day. Hey, instead of going house-hunting right now, why don't we go and see Becky and then that puppy?"

"Yes, all right. Good idea!"

"So, how do we find her?"

"Think?"

"Think, and that will find her?"

"Yes, it will, but what I meant was: think about how we found that puppy yesterday, and employ the same technique. Beck will be easier to find because she is your daughter, so you know already her vibration".

"Do I?"

"Yes, of course you do! You lived with her long enough".

"Yes, agreed, but I never once thought about how she resonated... that would have been a bit weird, if you ask me".

"People are only ten percent conscious. You do know it, trust me. Just think of Becky, and will yourself beside her. We'll both go".

"Do you think that I might get lost?"

"No, silly! You can't get lost! You would just will yourself to be back here, or with me!

"See! That wasn't difficult, was it? She's picking the kids up from school. Let's stand over the road and watch. She doesn't know that we're here".

"They look well, don't they? It seems they've gotten over my death already…"

"Hey! That's selfish. If they have, you should be glad about it. Watch this, I'll wait for her to finish crossing the street first… Becky! Ooh, Becky", she said waving a hand above her head. Becky turned in their direction, and stopped, seeming to squint at them.

They distinctly heard her say, 'Mam and Dad? Is that you?"

"Go on, answer the poor girl!"

"I heard her but I didn't see her lips move. Shall I speak like you did, or just think it?"

"Telepathy or speech, it doesn't matter. Just hurry".

"Yes, it's us, darling. We just came to see how you are". They watched a few tears run down her cheeks. "What's the matter, Mum?" asked Becky's older child.

"She's thinking of granddad again, aren't you Mum?" replied the younger one.

"Yes, my dears. I was thinking of your Nain and Taid… I thought I… never mind. Get in the car, we've got to get home early this evening. Your Dad's bringing someone special home from work for dinner, so I want you to eat your tea early, and then go to your rooms early tonight… and stay there!"

"Yes, Mum", they both replied together. Beck looked at her parents again as she got behind the wheel, but wasn't sure whether she could see them or not. "Bye-bye, Mam and Dad, I hope you're well".

"Why don't we go with them?" asked Willy.

"No, not in a car. It's not a good idea. Imagine, she's driving along. She looks in the rear-view mirror to overtake, and she sees the pair of us smiling back at her! No, you have to be careful, you could cause an accident".

"I suppose you're right again. Take care of yourself, darling!" said Willy sadly as they watched her drive off. "Strange, isn't it, love? It was great to see them again, but it made all of us sad".

"Yes, but that answers your earlier question about whether she has got over your death, doesn't it? Come on, let's go cheer up ourselves and that little puppy! Do you remember where it lives?"

"Yes, in Splott. Could we just sort of fly over there? Its only thirty miles, and I'd like to get a look at the old scenery again".

"Of course, we can", she said taking his hand and smiling. "I'll be Wendy and you can be Peter Pan".

∞

"I really am torn between living in the city and the county side... Do you have a preference, my dear?"

"I'm like you. We lived on Bryn Teg for so long, didn't we? I loved our little cottage there and the privacy, but they aren't really issues here. To be truthful, I haven't had a place to call my own since I've been here, but then, it is perfectly easy to live like that.

"I suppose that if I had to say here or there, it would be in the country again. In a place just like our old one".

"Yes, I think that would be best too. I don't suppose there are any rules about moving, are there? I mean, if we change our minds, we can just up-sticks and go?"

"Absolutely, although there would not be any sticks to up".

"Oh, well, in that case, it's a no-brainer! The countryside here we come! On the windward side of the hill facing the mountains?"

"Yes, please. With a garden front and back, and a winding road down to the local pub, so that you can play darts with your oppos".

"I haven't felt much like going to the pub since I've been here..."

"Ooh! You've been living in one!"

"Yes, we both have, but how many times have I sneaked downstairs for a swift one?"

Life in Annwn

"Yes, all right, I'll give you that. You have been pretty good…"

"Never! Not once have I gone down for a pint".

"No, that's true. You are showing some improvement…"

"One day you'll pay me a compliment and I'll drop down dead with shock!" Then he realised what he had said and began to smile. "Or do you say, 'be reborn on the Surface?"

They were both laughing now. "We don't say any such thing!"

"Well, you know what I mean anyway. It was lovely to play with that little puppy again today. Do you know, I think he was really pleased to see us. Do you know his name?"

"How would I know his name? He probably doesn't even know his own man-given name yet, and I don't speak fluent canine!"

"No, nor do I, though I have always had a special rapport with dogs… and sheep".

"And all other animals…"

"Thank you, dear. Yes, I like to think so".

"See you didn't undergo and cataclysmic event".

"Pardon? You've lost me".

"You said that if I ever paid you a compliment… well, I just did about animals, and nothing happened".

"No, it didn't, did it?" he said beaming from ear to ear, "But you've become a lot cheekier, since you've been here, my girl. I've a good mind to…"

"To what? You wouldn't dare!" she said defiantly leaning over towards him with a smile on her face.

"No, you're right. I wouldn't. I like the new cheeky you".

"Independent, not so much cheeky".

"Yes, all right. I like the more independent you, even if you are a bit cheeky too sometimes. You remind me of when we were younger … When we were teenagers courting. You had the same streak in you then…"

"Did I?"

"Yes, and I loved it in you. I suppose life just wears us all down, until we are only interested in getting through the day. It's a shame... Did I change as well?"

"I have always loved you".

"That's not what I asked though".

"Perhaps, you became a bit grumpier, a bit staid, but you were just getting on with it too".

"Yes, and neither of us noticed the change taking place, and neither of us did anything about it. Shame, eh?"

"She put her hands on his shoulder, hung off him and let out a deep sigh. "Don't worry about it, Willy. That was then and now is now".

"It's that type of phrase that confuses me again. We can go back into the past and forward into the future, so then could be now too..."

"No. We can go back into the past, or we can just watch a kind of film and it - The Akashic Record. If we are in the past, we can come back to the present, which from the perspective of the past is the future. However, from that perspective, some of the future has already happened - ie the bit from the time we decided to visit to the the time we decided to go back. That has already happened, so we can go there... we can return to our own time.

"What we cannot do, is travel to a time in the future that has not happened to us yet, although that doesn't stop someone from the future who has already experienced it coming back to visit us - we just wouldn't be able to accompany them back to their present, because that would be our future.

"Is that any clearer?"

"As clear as a muddy pool in a thunderstorm, but I'm sure that it's just me".

"OK. Simply put, you cannot change anything in the past, you can only visit someone else's past, and you cannot visit any future that you haven't already taken part in. Is that any better?"

"It's short - that's something! I'll try to remember it and think about it later".

"It all has to do with Karma. You cannot change anyone's Karma but your own, and then only by rightful deeds, speech and thought, which are basically the same thing anyway".

"Yes, OK. Will Kiddy come to join us in our cottage?"

"I should think so".

"We could turn it into a rescue home for traumatised animals".

"That would be a lot of animals…"

"Yes, dogs then… or dogs from South Wales".

"If you just said our old county of Gwent, you would have your hands full, but I like it. You're thinking along the right lines now. Let's go and find our cottage".

They travelled around a little, and visited dozens of excellent locations, but all of a sudden, Willy grabbed Sarah's shoulders. "I just had a thought!"

"Yes, it looked as if something happened to you…"

"What are we looking for? … Something like our old cottage, right?" He watched Sarah catch on. "Well, I bet that Becky hasn't sold it yet, so why don't we take vacant possession and claim Squatters' Rights!"

"Yes, we could have a word with Becky and ask her not to sell, and even if she had to, it wouldn't matter, because ghosts live side by side with Surface Dwellers all over the place. Let's go and see what state it's in".

They stood before it arm in arm, and both felt incredibly sad. The house looked sad too… sad and lonely… as if its only friends had died and it was all on its own. The boarding over the windows, made it look wounded. The rear view was no better, so they tentatively entered their old love nest through the kitchen wall.

To their mutual delight, the place was unoccupied. In fact, everything was as Willy remembered it that afternoon when he had gone out to tend the now overgrown gardens, except that his plate had been washed up and the stereo had been turned off.

"Wow! It looks like a shrine", he whispered.

"More evidence that she misses her father", said Sarah softly with a hint of reproach for his having doubted her. "That settles it then we'll move back in here".

"Yes, ma'am! I can hardly wait! Kiddy! Where are you, old girl?" and they snatched her walk through the wall towards them, panting, her tail beating wildly.

"It's almost like old times!" he grinned and hugged Sarah close.

Life in Annwn

6 THE SURFACE

"Let's do this place up a bit, shall we, Willy? It's awfully gloomy with those shutters over the windows. It's not like being in our beautiful, old cottage at all". They were sitting in their respective armchairs on either side of the fireplace. He stared at her.

"I'd love to, my dear, but are you sure that I can wield a hammer or a crowbar?"

"I am sure that you cannot, but I am also sure that you don't need to. You just want to not see them and they will vanish. They are not there for me, but I didn't know whether they were for you. Just saying, my dear".

"Well, you picked up on my thoughts perfectly. I was sitting here thinking how dingy it was, but I didn't want to ruin it for you by complaining. After all, we've only been here ten minutes, er, a short time - drat, I'll never get used to time here, or there, or wherever we are... Anyway, I just wanted to enjoy the moment of being with you again in our old cottage".

"That's a lovely thing to do and say, but try it. Just wish the shutters away and let the sun shine in, and later, we'll bank up a fire like we used to, sit here and read..."

"and I'll chop some logs and bring in a scuttle of coal!"

Willy turned to face the bay window, and no sooner had he thought about it, than the sun came streaming in through the net curtains, highlighting motes of dust on its way. "Amazing! We could be back thirty or forty years ago and I would never have known".

"We would have had Becky running around getting into all sorts of mischief, and I would have had to be thinking about dinner…"

"And I would have been contemplating a snooze, if it was a Sunday, otherwise I wouldn't have even been here!"

"And I would probably have been doing some knitting or darning… Those wellies of yours were always wearing holes in your socks…"

"Yes, good old days!" said Willy. Sarah just looked at him and nodded smiling.

"Can you feel that, Willy?" she asked rubbing her stomach.

"I can feel something, but I don't know where or what it is". He craned his neck.

"Yes, you might hear it rather than feel it… or both. Any idea what it is?"

"No, it's not unpleasant, but it pulls at your concentration a little…"

"… like the house phone ringing in another room?"

"Yes! I don't want to be bothered with it. What is it?"

"It's Becky thinking about us… she's crying in the house alone…"

"We have to go to her, but how do you know all that?"

"Practice. I know her vibration, and I just went to see her for a second… of Surface time!"

"Well let's go and comfort her. What are we waiting for?"

"Yes, we will go, but to answer you properly, it's just like with a crying baby… you want them to learn to do without you, and that is very hard for a mother, but it is better for the baby. Still, let's go".

They stood In the garden and peered through the wall, so that there was no chance of their daughter becoming aware of their presence. She was sitting at the kitchen table, her head on her arms, crying. "The poor girl", said Willy softly, "I had no idea that she would be so affected by my, or our, I suppose, death. I knew that she missed you terribly. You were always very close".

"The famous mother and daughter bond… but she was always Daddy's little girl too".

"I feel ashamed that I never noticed that. Isn't there anything we can do?"

"We can try to talk to her, to show her that we have not abandoned her. I'm pretty certain that she was aware of us in the pub after your funeral".

"Yes, I think she was too. Come on then. I'm guessing that you've done this sort of thing before". She fixed him with a steady gaze that seemed to hold some mockery.

"Really?" she said eventually.

"Oh, with me and Becky when you passed over, I suppose?"

"Duh, come on, Willy… Sit over there opposite me. Becky! Becky, cariad… it's your mother and father. Can you hear me?" She nodded at Willy.

"Becky, don't cry, love. We're still here with you… we haven't left you on your own… We still care very much…"

"Mam? I miss you and Da so-ooo much. I wish you and Da were still here. I'm lost without you…" and her crying became louder and more heart-wrenching. Tears trickled from Willy's eyes and he put his hand on Becky's shoulder without thinking about it. Becky froze visibly and looked up. "Mam, Da, are you here? I thought I saw you in the Red Dragon after Da's funeral, but John says I'm talking rubbish. I'm so confused. If it wasn't for the boys… I, I don't know what I'd do. I can't bear it alone".

"You're not alone, my dear, Da and I are always near by". Willy rubbed her shoulder.

"Of course, we are, darling. You only have to think of us and we will be there with you. I promise". She looked him full in the face, he tapped her shoulder again and then removed his hand to the table top. "Your mother's here too, sitting opposite me". However, Becky hadn't seen him and was only vaguely aware of distant voices. She couldn't hear exactly what they were saying. She picked up her empty coffee mug and added it to the breakfast things, then she took a glass from the wall unit and filled it with white wine from the fridge. She took a slug, topped it up and returned to her chair. Sarah looked at Willy, turned the corners of her mouth down, and wagged her finger at him, warning him not to reproach his daughter.

"We are here, Becky. You were right in the pub that afternoon. You did see us… we were there. We were there for you… and your family. Look at us, cariad". She covered Becky's right hand with hers, and nodded to Willy, who did the same to her left.

Becky looked slowly from her left to her right. "I can hear something or someone, but I'm so confused that I haven't a clue whether my mind is playing tricks on me. I so want it to be you that I'm hearing, Mam and Da. Please let it be you! It would make such a difference to me, and I do believe that it's possible. All those books that Da and I read, and the talks we had with Gareth and Emma… I know that it is possible, but I don't know whether I can do it alone…"

Sarah looked at Willy again, still with a sad face. "You were easier to convince, Willy, but Becky has less self-confidence, I'm afraid. That's not unusual though. It just means that we have to work harder, and be more patient".

"Well, I have all the time in the world if it will help our poor daughter. Could we encourage her to talk to Gareth and Emma? I'm sure that they could help convince her that she is capable of talking to us alone".

"We have two ways of trying that: asking Gareth and Emma to contact her, and keeping on putting the idea in her mind. Talking to Gareth and Emma would work more quickly".

"Yes, I can see that. Let's spend a bit more time here and then go to see Emma".

"OK".

∞

"Thank you for seeing us at such short notice, Gareth", said Sarah when they had located Gareth in The Sanctuary in their garden, where they met individuals when the church wasn't open.

"Oh, the pleasure is all mine, honestly. It's great to see you both again. Emma said that she will be here as soon as she can. How is Becky doing. I haven't seen her since your funeral, Willy".

"No, we have just left her. She may need some help… from friends that she can talk to easily. We weren't getting through to her very clearly".

"Sure, we'd be honoured to help. That's part of our purpose for setting up The Sanctuary really".

"Yes, it provides a very useful service. We will continue to try to get through to her, but one of the problems is that her husband, John, keeps telling her that she's imagining it all"

"A common problem, I'm afraid".

"Oh, yes. A less confident person will not want to look stupid to his or her peers… I know the feeling", said Willy. "When I started after my Near-death Experience a lot of people down the pub laughed at me, but I stuck with it".

"But you were living alone, Willy, and I was there almost all the time. Now, we need to be there for Becky. John is a big influence on her and he is sceptical. She faces a more difficult time of it than you did".

"Yes, I can see that, Sarah, so we have to give her more support… and if Gareth and Emma will help too, we should be able to prevent Becky from thinking she's going mad".

"… or being persuaded that she's going mad!"

"Well, Emma and I will be only too pleased to do all we can, of course we will. In fact, I'll ask Emma to phone her this evening to see when it would be convenient to meet up".

"Thank you, Gareth. We appreciate that, don't we, Sarah?"

"Yes, very much so. Thank you, Gareth, and thank Emma for us too, please". Willy gave her a quizzical look, having expected to wait for Emma. "Until soon" and they both left.

"Why didn't we wait for Emma?"

"There was no need. He will arrange that. We can go back to Becky".

∞

"That was an eventful day, or whatever you want to call it, wasn't it,

Sarah?" said Willy stretching his legs out towards the roaring fire that they had imagined into the fireplace. Sarah put her book on loneliness down and looked at him.

"I know that you've still having problems with Time, so you call it what you want and I'll convert it if necessary... a bit like when Britain changed the currency. Yes, it was a very satisfying 'day'. The goal is to have that warm feeling of having been useful every time you have to take a break to recharge".

"... or when we went metric".

"Pardon?"

"You were talking about the confusion when Britain dropped 'Pounds, Shillings and Pence' in favour of a decimal currency... it was the same when we went metric. Some of the old guys down the pub still use the old Imperial measurements. You remember old Kenny the chippy? When his boss announced that the firm was going to adopt the new metric industry standard, he scoured the builders' merchants for Imperial tape measures and bought the lot! Then he stood on his union right not to have to buy new tools just to comply with the new standard! The wily old fox had enough old tapes to last him out to retirement, so he never had to accept or give a metric measurement in his life!

"It is so nice to be with you again in our old cottage. I would never have thought it could be like this ever again. Life here is satisfying and enjoyable in a way that I could not have imagined. I'm afraid that I was one of those who thought that life in Heaven had to be boring. I mean, I knew that it was supposed to be perfect, that's what we're told, aren't we? And if it's perfect, then you can have what you want and there is no strife... and I suppose that that part is true, but I never foresaw the rest of it... I had no idea about the work that goes on in Heaven, or Annwn, I suppose I should be calling it in Wales... It's just not like I imagined. Who would have thought that even if you can have anything you want... in a material sense, that that wouldn't necessarily make you happy?"

"It was the same for me. It is the same for most people, I think. That's why so many people come here and just stop. They literally just stop doing anything! Like a train at the terminal station. We are not taught properly, and we are taught by people who know as little about these things as we did".

"The blind leading the blind".

"Yes, unfortunately. At least, in these matters. And the ones who profess to know The Truth are vilified in the media by people who don't want you to know The Truth, because organised religions teach obedience to Caesar. They uphold the status quo... The government, the upper and ruling classes together with their state religion work together to maintain their privilege, not necessarily for the benefit of the masses or to educate them".

"I've never heard you speak like that before, Sarah. I'm the Trotskyist..."

"You were the Red in my bed, not under it. Politics didn't interest me then, though I did listen to what you said. Surface politics doesn't interest me now either, but the human condition does, and I am learning that that is mostly a controlled environment like a farm or a zoo, and the zoo keepers are the ruling class, in cahoots with the top politicians and others, whose philosophy seems to be 'If you can't beat them, join them'. I just don't agree with constraining people's right to self-development". Willy started clapping.

"I am not being patronising, honest. I am in awe. You are inspiring... truly inspirational, my dear!"

"Thank you. You never stop learning... or no-one should... even in eternity, stagnation is a waste of time", she said grinning.

Willy roared with laughter and started clapping again.

"I love it!" he exclaimed. "I love it and I love you! I haven't had such a good laugh for ages, and, it's on a serious subject. That would never have happened down the Red Dragon! Not in a million years! Life in Annwn's not so boring as people might think.

"One question though, since we're being so serious, why is Annwn so different from Heaven?"

"It's not. It's exactly the same... 'A rose by any other name is still a rose', but when the early Roman Christians came over and found the Celts praying to their God who lived underground, or Under the Mountain, they thought they were devil-worshippers, and persuaded the church hierarchy to teach their Flock that the true God lived in Heaven, which was in the sky. So, gradually, people preyed to God in Heaven, in the sky, rather than Annwn which was underground".

"How can you persuade ethical people who know better? Surely, they would have just told them to sod off?"

"How naive… They bought off the corruptible, and killed off the ethical. The same way that conquerors always do. That's how Christianity became a tool of the rulers, or the state, as they put it euphemistically".

"You would be marked down as a Trot, if we lived on the Surface in bodies".

"Who cares?"

7 FAMILY AND OLD FRIENDS

"Yesterday was fun, rewarding and disappointing all at once", said Willy, his head on his hand, lying on the bed next to Sarah. "You can really pack a lot into a day in Annwn, can't you?"

"Yes, for sure, but what you call 'a day' is the twenty-four-hour period you were used to on the Surface. You are calling the period between resting 'a day', but that is not always the same length of 'time'. For example, you could probably do something easy like going for a walk for many Surface years without becoming 'tired', but a much shorter period of emotionally-draining work might make you want to rest. Do you see? The active period between resting are not of equal length. It makes relating our 'time' to theirs extremely difficult, especially for the newcomer, even though they have been here before. Indeed, even though they have spent much more time here than anywhere else.

"For example, you have rested six times, so you probably calculate that you have been here a week of Surface time, but it could easily have been several months or even years!

"It's one of the reasons why the Surface Dwellers don't see their dearly departed for quite a long time after they have passed away... and that is one of the reasons why people say, 'I don't believe in life after death, because my whatever promised to come back and tell me that there really was an Afterlife'. The simple truth is that that person didn't realise how quickly an infinite amount of time in Eternity can pass..."

"... because they are comparing apples with oranges!?"

"Exactly! By George, I think he's got it! To be fair though, it is difficult to understand... and to explain".

"Hear! Hear! I can vouch for that".

"Don't worry about it! I keep saying that. You are doing very well!"

Life in Annwn

"Thanks. I think that it's the phrase you've used most often to me since I've been here".

"Perhaps, but I don't think so. Anyway, do you have any ideas about what you want to do next?"

"Well, I thought we could check on Becky and the puppy again, and then perhaps, look up some old friends…"

"In the Dragon?"

"Yes, but it's not as if I can have a couple of pints with them, is it?"

"I'm not criticizing. Or I didn't mean it to come over that way anyway… Yes, we could do that. Lead the way…"

"Becky first, I think", he said and was gone. Sarah caught up with her husband in the garden again. "She looks a lot better toda… I mean, this time. She's doing the dishes… still got a glass of wine though…"

"That's not too much to be concerned about, Willy. A lot of middle-class housewives drink a few glasses of wine during the day. She looks a lot happier. That's the main thing. Let's go inside and see if we can talk to her". They passed through the wall and stood a metre or so to her right - near the dish rack, but she didn't notice them.

"Afternoon, Becky. It's your Mam and Da. How are you this afternoon?"

"Mam, is that you? I so want to talk to you, and Dad, if he's with you".

"We're both here, dear". Willy stood back to watch the scene unfold and give his wife more room. Sarah put her arms around her daughter and hugged her. They both started to sob gently. "We're here for you, Becky. Never doubt that. Listen to your heart, not other people's heads. Believe in what you feel, not what you read. I am here, my dear, feel my loving arms around you…"

"Yes, Mam, I can hear you, I'm pretty sure that I can". She stepped back and looked hard at her mother, but it was her father that she saw over Sarah's shoulder. He noticed and waved back.

"Dad? I can see you, Da! Is Mam here too? I think she is". William walked towards her.

"She is standing two feet in front of you, cariad".

Sarah squinted, then cocked her head, and then took a pace backwards. "Mam!" she blurted out and they both lurched forward into each other's arms, but Becky did not have the sensation of touch. "I can see you Mam, but Dad more easily, and I can near you both now that I'm sure that it is you speaking, but I can't feel you touching me".

William sat down at the table as before, and the two ladies followed suit. "I had better sit down before I fail down. Oh, what a comfort it is to know that you are still around! The boys will be so pleased too! And as for John, well, he can stick it in his pipe and smoke it! What a nice surprise this is!"

Willy tapped her hand and smiled, but her mother said, "Don't use us as a weapon in you war against your husband, please, Becky. That's not the right thing to do. Tell him by all means, but not in a spiteful way, please".

Becky tended to look more at her father because he was more clearly defined. His human form was quite crisp, although he looked much younger than she could remember ever having seen him, but there was a coloured glow around him, which she guessed was his Aura, since she had read so much about it. However, when she regarded her mother, the image of her young body blurred into her Aura, making it far less clear. It was more transparent too. With practice, she found that looking slightly past her mother produced the best result. It was a little like watching a large fish two feet deep in a swift-flowing river.

"We were concerned about you, cariad", said her father soothingly. "We were a close family, though we didn't all show it openly, and we were worried about how you were taking my Departure from The Surface".

"Sorry, Dad... What was that?"

"Your father is saying that we were worried about how you were dealing with his passing away".

"Oh... It was a massive blow. First Mam and then you. It was just too much. I don't think I have been coping very well. I've been neglecting the house and my appearance... not the kids though... although I'm sure that they must have noticed a difference… and as for John, to be honest, and I don't know whether it's his fault or mine, but, well, we just can't seem to stop fighting… The kids must have noticed.

"And I've been hitting the bottle… only white wine, but too much… I know that…" Sarah and Willy exchanged meaningful glances.

"Don't worry about that now, dear", said her mother. "Draw strength from the knowledge that we have not left you alone, and never will. If you need us, you only have to think of us, and we will be with you".

"We are in the cottage now, Becky. You can find us in our old home", whispered Willy. Sarah looked at him and transferred the thought to him to leave for home, and they vanished.

Becky saw them leave, but was not disappointed, rather, she was elated that she was now certain that she was not alone and that she could contact them whenever she wanted. She went back to the washing up with renewed vigour and cheer. She was looking forward to talking to her children before their father got home from work.

∞

Sitting on the grass in their back garden, Willy felt happy and relaxed. "I'm so pleased that we have cheered Becky up… She was going down hill".

"Mmm, it is often the way. People grieve for their dearly departed in private, because they think that it shows weakness. It's also ironic that people pity the deceased, when it is they themselves who are worse off.

"Nobody who passes on from The Surface goes to a worse place".

"Yet those left behind say silly things like, 'Why did he have to die?', and, 'She was only twenty-five, she had all her life before her!' If only they knew what nonsense they were spouting".

"Willy! You were probably the same before you learned better. People have to learn for themselves, especially in the West - many Eastern and African religions are closer to The Truth. Christianity has been well and truly hijacked though".

"It's a shame that the Hippies succumbed to the Establishment, isn't it?"

"In a way, yes, but for some reason, they didn't bother to impart the knowledge that they had learned to their children. The post-Hippy kids were the worst cooks ever!"

"There were lots of things that they had learned from their parents that they did not pass on, not only cooking. The post-war work ethic vanished too. The boom years of the Fifties, Sixties and Seventies persuaded people that no-one would have to work hard again".

"That is not exactly what the government told us, but they did promise that robots and computers would take over much of the manual work, so that man would not have to work hard again. It was lies. People still have two or three jobs per household and are struggling to pay off their debt".

"Our lives in the hills and mountains didn't change much though, did they?"

"No! Computers can't hill farm sheep… and nor can robots. I doubt whether they ever will be able to either".

"I shouldn't think so either, my dear".

"I'd like to go to the Dragon and see who's about…"

"Why don't you?"

"Aren't you coming as well?"

"I don't see the point, love. I only ever went in there half a dozen times in my life. I doubt that anyone would even know who I am".

"Just for moral support then… I'm a bit nervous about going on my own…"

"Why? You've known most of the locals since you were schoolboys!"

"Yes, but they've never seen me quite like this before".

"I don't know about that. Who's to say that you didn't know some of them before you were reborn? … or that you didn't go Astral Travelling together sometimes? You don't remember the half of what you've got up to.

"Not only that, but I knew you before were reborn, and nothing that you've seen or done so far, you haven't seen or done many times before.

"Really, this is all old hat to you, but you haven't broken through yet".

"How do you mean?"

"Well, like the amnesiac... sometimes, something happens that brings all the old memories flooding back".

"Yes, I see..."

"That's probably why Becky said that she could see you more clearly than me. Your vibrations are lower than mine, because you are still strongly linked with The Surface... much more than I am at any rate".

"Because I have just come from there?"

"Possibly... maybe even probably, but it could be a link to someone or something that you feel strongly".

"I can't imagine what that would be except Becky and the kids... I mean you and Kiddy are here... we're living in our cottage on our hill. I can't think what that could be".

"No, well, it doesn't matter. It will wear off. Now go and see your friends in the pub".

"Wow! I bet that's the first time you've ever said that to me!"

"Well, you'd better go now then, before I change my mind, hadn't you?"

"Are you sure you won't come with me?"

"Positive. Now go!"

"Yes, ma'am", he said saluting, and vanished.

No sooner had he left, than Sarah disappeared too leaving Kiddy alone basking in the glow of the fire on the rug.

∞

Willy stood outside his old local and stared in through the window. There were a fair few in there, so he picked a quiet corner and put himself in it. He was four or five yards from the bar on the one hand and the same from a group of old men playing cards on the other. Frank was behind the bar idly cleaning glasses while waiting for custom. He sat on the nearest chair for no good reason and waited for someone to notice him.

Nothing had changed in the old place, he noted, but then wondered why it would have in the few weeks since he had passed over. If it was a few weeks - he couldn't really be certain how long ago it was.

He scanned the bar for the racing calendar that had always hung near the hatch. It was October 19th. judging by the days that had been crossed off, and he had passed away on August 14th. He was surprised that nine weeks had passed already - about three times longer than he had guessed.

Not that it made the slightest drop of difference. His old window seat opposite the bar became free, so he willed himself into for old time's sake. It felt comfortable and familiar. As he settled in, he noticed a plaque on the wall. It was shiny brass, about the size of a letter plate, and the inscription read, 'Willy Jones' seat. Gone but not forgotten. Loved by All. RIP'.

It mesmerized him. He never would have guessed in his wildest dreams that anyone would have done that for him. 'Must have been Becky, love her' he thought.

Willy wasn't disappointed that no-one saw him sitting in his corner and when people did look, he put it down to their idle scanning of the room, and he was right to do so. He did feel happy there though and decided to return from time to time.

He willed himself home and into his armchair by the fire. He leaned forward, patted the dog and said, "Where's your mother, old girl? Popped out a moment, has she? Well, we'll just sit here and wait for her together, shall we?"

Life in Annwn

8 INCREASING INVOLVEMENT

"Have you noticed that you are not needing to rest so much any more, Willy? You are coming out of the Circadian Cycle".

"Yes, time seems to be expanding. I remember when I and others used to wish that there were more than twenty-four hours in a day, well, now, sometimes, there seem to be".

"Yes, well, the Circadian Rhythm still has twenty-four, of course, but you are not following that very closely any more. One 'day', you will hardly remember that it exists since you might not even be living near Earth".

"That would be weird, wouldn't it?"

"It would for me, but I have only ever lived here. I don't know about you. I mean, I knew you in Annwn before we were reborn, but I don't know what you did before I met you".

"I don't know either…"

"Yes, but it will come back to you. Anyway, I've been thinking. Becky is used to the fact that we are still around now. She sees us clearly and talks to us quite naturally, so why don't we try to build on that?"

"In what way, my dear?"

"Well, the way here is to see an opportunity and take it forward… not like before, for profit and gain over others, but for the benefit of others and ultimately everyone - not even only mankind. For the benefit of Spirit, if you like, because that's what it all comes down to.

"If you can raise awareness in a small household in Brecon, that will raise the awareness in Wales, in the UK, in Europe, in the World, the Galaxy, the Universe and so on and so on ad infinitum. Who knows who will ultimately benefit from Becky's increase in Spiritual knowledge. Almost certainly her sons, and perhaps, John… and who knows whom they will meet in the course of their lives on Earth and whom they will influence to do better and what effect that might have on humanity.

"It is not given to many to make a huge difference in the world, but we can all help set the wheels of change in motion".

"They are wonderful sentiments, Sarah. Humbling… so what are you thinking of?"

"I was thinking that we should help Becky Increase her Spiritual knowledge and further her psychic development".

"Yes, that sounds great. I might even pick up a few tips myself!"

"Yes, that's what I was thinking too. I always try to kill two birds with one stone. That way, if one objective fails, the other may not. You will remember though, and while we are reminding you, Becky might as well sit in and learn something too".

"Fine. You lead and I'll follow".

"OK, let's go!"

It was afternoon, and Becky was drinking coffee in their living room when they arrived on the sofa near her.

"Good afternoon, cariad", said Willy. "You are looking well!"

"Hello, Mam, hello, Dad".

"Becky," continued her father, "do you remember the books we used to read together, and the exercises we used to do?"

"Yes…"

"Do you still do that?" asked Sarah.

"No, not really, Mam. I've been distracted recently, and not having Da to learn with, I've sort of let it slide".

"Yes, that's what we thought. Would you take it back up again if we helped you?"

"Yes, I'd really like that. The three of us working together? Yeah, I'd love it. I miss you both so much".

"OK, we can start as soon as you like. You have to work out a time when it is convenient for you - like say, Wednesday evening at seven - and keep that time free every week. You should present yourself at the meeting relaxed, calm and not tired. If you can do that, we'll do the rest.

"Choose the time wisely and let us know. You only have to think it to us"

"How did it go with John and the children?"

"Oh, I didn't tell the children about you... not yet anyway, but I will. John became a little angry and said something sarcastic about seeing Spirits though a bottle. I didn't resist. I couldn't be bothered. I hope that's all right".

"You play it however you see fit, Becky. We will work to your pace".

"OK, thanks, but why is a regular time so important"

"Because it helps you to focus and prepare for the meeting, and it allows us to plan our time as well"

"Is it busy in Annwn then? I always thought that the Deceased had nothing to do... that they led the life of Leisure and Luxury".

"There is a bit more to it than that, but we can make time to fit in with your schedule".

"I see. OK, I'll be in touch soon once I've thought about a permanent regular time".

∞

"So, what are you going to start Becky off with at her first meeting?" asked Willy.

"Well, I know that you and she did some work before, but we don't know how much she remembers about that, so, we'll just start again from the beginning. There is no hurry, we will see how quickly she learns whether that is because she remembers from before she was reborn or because she has only a short time to devote to her studies because of her worldly commitments".

"So, yoga and meditation?"

"Yes. Shall we go and check up on on your puppy?"

"Yes, OK, but he's not really a puppy any more. In fact, I use him to judge how long I've been here - a few months now, I reckon. I think that he's doing so well that we could reduce our visits to him and look around for a couple more".

"That's the way! Share the love. There is nothing wrong with making more lasting relationships, but, in general, we help get a soul back on his feet and then move on".

"Like aid workers on t The Surface?"

"I suppose so, but it's not really the same… we don't have a network of office staff to support".

"But the foot soldiers need to be organised by someone or nothing would happen. It'd be chaos!"

"Yes, you are right, but such a high percentage of every donation goes in administration".

"Where there's money involved, there will always someone be making a profit. It's the way of the world".

"You said it, but it is not the only way. The problem is that it is the only way that works well with the system they have in the West. People need to change, and they do over time. The only thing is that by the time that happens, most people have moved on to another incarceration and possibly even a different planet or dimension. Earth is a low-grade school and it's purpose is to be such".

"So we shouldn't criticise people who are there because they are only learning how to behave?"

"That is a way of looking at it. At least they have realised that they are imperfect and so have chosen to go back to school. Some never do. Some have been squandering their existence for ever, or as near as you can get, and they are still so conceited and arrogant that they think they are good enough as they are!"

"I don't think I've met anyone like that, have I?"

"No, you wouldn't have. They have mostly never left Annwn, or only once or twice and didn't like it. You wouldn't meet them on this Plane either because they are from a lower vibration and wouldn't like it here".

"So, lower than those medieval soldiers in the inn? Oh, yes! Much lower than them! You met those people on this Plane. They may be a bit slow on the uptake, or lazy, or perhaps they have only recently admitted to themselves that they are dead, but at least they are comfortable here. That alone tells you something about them.

"Do you remember the pub analogy I gave you before?"

"Yes. Some people feel happier in a dive, others in a posh bar, and they rarely mix, and never on a regular basis".

"Yes. You would not feel happy being around such Souls, but we do go down to talk to them to try to make them see that there is more to life than what they have".

"Like the Salvation Army?"

"A little bit, but we don't collect money from people whose lifestyle we despise. We only try to help".

"Money is necessary on The Surface".

"Money is necessary because mankind has made it necessary. It was not inevitable, and it could be a phase, but we will have to wait and see what they want for a future".

"I would never have expected to hear you talk like this when we lived on The Surface?"

"No, but from here you get a better perspective than from the hill our little cottage is on. Education helps too, and here you have the opportunity to learn The Truth about any subject - not just someone's opinion. The Truth, first time round".

"You will have to show me how that works. There are a few things that I would like to know more about".

"Any time. You only have to ask"

"Seek and Ye shall find! Eh?"

"Exactly! When the pupil is ready, the teacher will appear".

"Do you think that I am being a bit slow in taking up the reins again? I mean, I have been back here for three or four months now, and I am still asking how things work".

"It doesn't matter how long it takes, Willy. Really, it doesn't".

"So, why do I feel like a dunce?"

"Probably because you are inquisitive and you have chosen to hang around with me". She smiled, but meant it.

"I haven't met anyone yet, have I? I mean, not really. I don't have anyone else to compare myself with…"

"No, but that is not a bad thing at this stage. You shouldn't be judging yourself against others. Their rate of progress is their business, and yours is yours, and yours alone. However, if you want to progress, you know what to do".

"Yes, so for now, I'll just keep asking questions, if I'm not boring you".

"No, you are not boring me. It is a privilege to be asked to help".

"Thank you, Sarah. You just said that I have you. Isn't it normal for marriages to last afterwards… after, you know?"

"If you said that more than fifty percent makes normal, then no, it is not normal. Not many remain married, but a lot stay friends… or friendly".

"Really? That surprises me!".

"Why? I should imagine that it's about a quarter, who actively seek each other out. Many could wait to be free from their spouse. Others got remarried before they passed away. Some found more loving partners or relationships here, and yet others returned to partners from before they were reborn…"

"That sounds a bit weird!"

"Like I said, there are all kinds here - even more than there are on The Surface. Don't forget, we have types who have never been there, types who are ready to go back, and those who will never go back because they are ready to move on to a higher level - a higher school, if you like".

"Yeah, I get it. Will I ever get to meet any of these other types?"

"Of course, if you like. Whenever you want".

"I've been thinking too. Didn't I have any friends from before I went to The Surface?"

"Yes, of course you did. I was one of them. We decided to go there together!"

"That's nice… reassuring. And the others?"

"You are still a bit 'dense' for some of them, and others are busy, but they do ask after you".

"Dense? Charming!"

"Yes, sorry, but you are still of a dense vibration, and some people have a problem with that… like talking to a foreigner who doesn't speak their language".

"That's not very nice of them, is it? They can't be bothered to stick with me and try…"

"They were mostly your friends… perhaps you have changed your mind about some of them after learning what you did on The Surface. Don't forget, you have just come back from university after completing a degree course, while most of them have been 'resting' here. Others are actually on The Surface at this moment.

"If you don't progress, you stand still, and if those around you are still moving forward, well, then, the chances are that you will grow apart, or not?"

"Yes, I suppose so. I've seen it happen many times in the village. Someone's kid goes off to university, but can't settle in the village again afterwards, because… well, I guess it's just like you said. He or she has improved him or herself while the villagers have stood still. I just didn't think that it would happen here too".

"Why ever not? Human nature is human nature, we don't become angels when we die! Vibration! Remember vibration! If the vibrations are compatible, people will feel comfortable, if not, then they will have to go where they do. And education and experience, similar things really, alter one's thought patterns and so one's vibrations. It's that simple".

"I see. Well, I don't want to give up on them that easily. I mean, we must have been friends at one time. I will have to meet them again one day".

"Of course. Why not? Loyalty is an admirable quality".

"Have you thought about going back, Sarah?"

"Sometimes. I am keen, but I wanted to talk to you first..".

"You put your life on hold to wait for me? Thank you".

"It was nothing, in the scheme of things. Think nothing of it".

"Oh, but I do. I appreciate it. So, if you want to be reborn, how do you go about it?"

"Oh, it is quite complicated, and usually takes a long time in Surface measurements. You could liken it to choosing a university degree course. However, you can can choose the length of the course and how deeply you want to go into your main subject, and how many side subjects you want to study. Once you have decided on that, then comes the difficult bit!

"Where best to study it. You have to work all that out first, but I have made it sound easy, believe me! Why are you thinking about going back already? Are you that unhappy being here with only me?"

"No, of course not! Never! I have missed you for decades, how can you think that?"

"I don't. I was just playing with you… You are so easy to wind up these days!"

"That is because the lovely Sarah that I remember from The Surface would not have pulled my leg as much as you do".

"Maybe the lovely Sarah that you knew here before we were reborn used to be exactly lime that, but didn't on The Surface, and now she does again because she is back to her old self. Perhaps she was nervous on The Surface and needed to go with someone who would give her support and encouragement, and maybe she was too in need of him to risk upsetting him".

"Is that true?"

"I'm not saying. A girl likes to have her secrets, but it might be. Perhaps that girl has learned to stand on her own two feet now, or perhaps she has learned that the man can take, or even could do with, a bit of leg-pulling".

"Perhaps, and would you go back there with that man again?"

"That would be telling, wouldn't it? Anything is possible".

"So, I have a chance then?"

"Oh, you have a chance… yes, you definitely have a chance".

9 HOLIDAYS

"You are doing well, Becky! Try to hold the headstand a few minutes longer. The Sirsasana sends extra blood and oxygen to the brain producing an increased ability to think and reason. Your record to date has been seven minutes in this position, but that is already double what you could manage last time. You will really feel the benefit of the Sirs asana, when you can hold the position for more than twenty minutes and carry out the Ujjayi pranayama at the same time., but don't worry about that, you're doing really well.

"Enough! I'm feeling dizzy!"

"You are not used to the extra capacity, but as you practice, you will be. Everything takes time. While your brain is still oxygen-rich, let's meditate on why you are doing these exercises. When you are finished, you will feel equal to any challenge for the rest of the day, but we will have left, so we will take our leave now.

"Go with God, beloved".

"See you soon, Becky. Well done".

"Bye Mam, bye Dad. Thanks for coming. It was great to see you again".

"I have a surprise for you, Willy, if you're interested".

"Yes, I like surprises!"

"Oh, I think that you'll like this one, but it is more of a suggestion than a surprise. How would you like to go somewhere?"

"Sure. Where? The inn, the pub, to see one of the puppies?"

"No, or yes, I mean if that's what you want, but I was thinking of going further afield than that".

"OK! Where?"

"Anywhere you like… and I literally mean anywhere on Earth or off".

"Off planet?"

"Yes".

"Like the Moon, or Mars?"

"Yes, or further. Anywhere".

"I'd love to, but I have no idea where. I've never been to any other planets before… have I?"

"Yes, you have. You just don't remember, that's all. We used to travel a lot before, though not so much when we were on The Surface. I don't remember why we stopped… too many other things on our minds, probably".

"OK, sure! I'm up for it. Are you saying that we can just go though? No preparations? No nothing?"

"Yes. What preparations do you want to make?"

"I don't know", he said after a little thought. "There is nothing, is there?" She shook her head slowly, smiling.

"Populated or unpopulated?"

"Mmm… would they speak English? No, eh?"

"No, but some peoples are so advanced that it doesn't matter what language you speak".

"But would I be able to understand them?"

"I don't know, probably not. I usually struggle, but it's not unlike going on holiday to France or Spain or somewhere like that for British people. It can be fun. You used to enjoy it".

"Did I? I suppose I can imagine that, but I don't feel up to it yet. Could we go somewhere beautiful where there aren't any people?"

"Yes, of course. Are you ready?"

"In for a penny…"

"Take my hand, darling".

They were above Earth's atmosphere almost instantaneously, doing their impression of Peter Pan and Wendy, and then they seemed to slow down, although, in reality, it was only the vast distance they were covering that made it appear so.

"The colours of the stars is so much more vibrant", he remarked. "You can't see them from Earth - they all look the same, don't they?"

"Yes, to the naked eye... I have never looked through a telescope, have you?"

"Only a small old brass one I found in a junk shop. You know the the type sailors used before binoculars became available".

They travelled on at they knew not what speed until Sarah pulled them up. What do you think of this one?"

"It's difficult to say from up here. Whatever you recommend".

"Come on down then!"

"What do you call this planet?"

"I personally call it Blogau Glas, but I don't know what other people call it, or even whether anyone else knows about it".

"Blodau Glas' - 'Blue Flowers', but why?"

"You'll see". Seconds later they were standing on the planet's surface ankle deep in luxurious blue grass.

"Wow. I have heard of the Blue Grass of Kentucky, but I doubt that it is as blue as this".

"It isn't. After I found this, I went to check, and Kentucky bluegrass is green, but it bears small blue flowers, which give a field of it a blue glow. This grass really is blue, a bright vibrant blue, but it's not only the grass that's blue".

"No, most of the trees and plants are blue too". "It's sort of funny on the eyes, isn't it? After a lifetime on a green planet, now everything that was green on Earth is blue... all the plant life anyway. It's a strange coincidence isn't it that 'glas' in Welsh can mean green or blue, so the plants here and on Earth would have the same name, well, description?"

"Not only in Welsh too. Many of the oldest languages use blue and green as the same word. Japanese did too... and the other Celtic languages, so you would have to say 'gass green' or 'sky blue' to get your meaning across..."

"That wouldn't work here though, because they're both, well, a shade of blue!"

"I looked up why grass is green on Earth, if you've interested".

"Yes, go on then".

"Well, it's not my subject, so I might have it wrong, but it has to do with Earth's Vegetation Red Edge. Our plants are green because they use chlorophyll, which is green, so they absorb blue, and especially red, reflecting back mostly green. I suppose that that means that these plants use a different system and so reflect blue, but I don't know why".

"I had no idea that you would have been so keen to look things up and check things out when we lived on our mountain".

"I didn't get a lot of time, did I? Not really. We were pretty remote… we didn't even have running water when we first moved in! Do you remember?"

"Yes, but the toilet was the worst!"

"It was nothing more than a smelly hole leading to a smelly pipe and an awfully smelly pit! Oh, my God!"

"What was the point in being curious in anything. We had no time, and even if we did find five minutes for leisure, we only had one book - The Bible that your Mam gave us…"

"Yes, no TV back then… a dodgy radio signal and definitely no Internet".

"It hadn't been invented, had it? It hadn't got to Brecon, in any case!"

They laughed and joked about the 'old days' and language and how redundant it was where they lived now, and walked many miles looking for plants and animals.

"I haven't been here often", said Sarah, but I have never seen any animals larger than butterflies. Then there are their caterpillars too, of course".

"There must be something else, surely?"

"I don't know. Look up there". Sarah pointed up into the branches of a large blue tree with oval leaves.

"Thousands of yellow butterflies!"

"Yes. Aren't they beautiful?"

"Ye, but if I saw those on a nature program on TV, I wouldn't be surprised".

"No, they could be Asian or African. They are four times the size of the biggest British butterflies, but not exceptional, but they are the only ones I've found".

"What, no spotted or silver ones?"

"Afraid not! No such luck", and they laughed and flopped down in the rich grass behaving more like young lovers on holiday for the first time alone.

While walking though a copse one day, Sarah stopped suddenly. "Did you feel that?"

"I felt something... like a tug at the clothing on my stomach, but not on my clothing. Strange".

"That is Becky getting ready for our next meeting and thinking about us. It is time to go back".

"But that means that we've been here for a week all ready!"

"Yes. It passes quickly, eh?"

"I should say so! I haven't enjoyed myself so much for..." he shook his head, "I don't know how long. Ages and ages... decades, scores of years. How did we let having fun like this slip through our fingers?"

"It's called life on Earth, darling. We did have fun like this when we were young. Remember our trips to Barry Island and Swansea?"

"Yes, the Mumbles... and Barry... they were good times, after the War... then the Seventies, we got married and it all changed".

"Don't say it like that, Willy. Marriage didn't change us... Responsibilities did, I think. We were carefree before we got married, and after it, well, we fell into the trap of complicating our lives... we started to want things".

"Our own house, more sheep, children, a car..."

"Yes, but don't blame Becky either. We wanted her and it's not a child's fault that they need things".

"No, I'm not blaming Becky, to be sure, I'm not, but she was one of those responsibilities that changed our easy lives. What with clothes, and then special clothes for school, and a car to take her down to the village school every morning and bring her back every evening..."

"I don't begrudge her any of that, Willy, do you?"

"No, but those things were factors in changing our previous way of life. No, I don't blame her for those things at all..."

"She has brought us so much happiness".

"I agree. I really do. But this is nice too... It's just a shame that a working-class couple can't have a life and a family. It seems that it has to be one or the other".

"I wouldn't change a minute of it. We have had a wonderful time together, or I have anyway. Come on, let's make a move".

"Don't go getting all upset. I am happy with the life we had together. I'm just saying that I enjoyed the freedom of our youth too. Honestly, dear. Let's not spoil the great week that we've had here on Blodau Glas".

"Yes, all right, dear, but we ought to be going anyway". Willy hugged his wife too him, but retained hold of one hand and they ascended into the atmosphere to begin their journey back to their mountain. Willy felt as if he were in the doghouse, but Sarah was not angry, only contemplating life.

"You didn't find anywhere to buy me an ice cream, Mam", he said trying to lighten the mood.

∞

At Becky's they continued with the Yoga Asanas and preceded and followed by Pranayama, but they also introduced meditation using the light of a candle as a focal point, nit unlike what Willy had taught her before. She was picking it all back up quite quickly.

When they had done enough, they sat down for a chat.

"We went away for a week's holiday!" said Willy, "I bet you'll never guess where we went".

"Ye, but before we get on to that. While we were away, we talked about the future, Becky. Didn't we, Willy?"

"Yes. We did indeed. Listen to this".

"We are very pleased with your progress, Becky. I know that you have covered a lot of this with hour father already, but even so, you are doing very well. So, we were wondering where you would like to go with all this new-found knowledge?"

"Go? I don't understand".

"What do you think you could best use it for?" asked Willy.

"I don't know. I have never thought about that. Why would I use it for anything?"

"Let me give you an example. I want to warn you that eldest child is developing an allergy towards some artificial sweeteners. I am not certain which ones as the allergy is not fully developed. However, it is something that he is showing a weakness towards, so you should be aware of it. I don't think that a doctor would be able to help yet, because the medical profession probably doesn't have equipment sensitive enough to detect it yet. You might be able to prevent the allergy from becoming real by ensuring that the food he consumes is free of all artificial sweeteners.

"Being able to help by giving such early warnings is a benefit of developing your higher senses".

"Yes, I would like to be able to help people like that…"

"Yes. I am sure that you would, but in a way, being able to pass on such helpful advice is an ego trip, isn't it? Depending upon the reason for giving the advice".

"Yes, I can see that", she replied, her crest falling rapidly.

"I could also tell you that your grandmother, my mother, told me to tell you that, and that she watches over her grandchildren every day at school. She says to tell you that they are good children… a credit to you and John".

"Nain Megan said that?" (Put in glossary).

"Yes. I am not telling you these things to polish my ego, but, in general, you have to be careful why you say these things. It is generally all right amongst loved ones. However, the most usual reason for giving such advice is to provide evidence of life after death, because if people are convinced of that fact, they will be far less likely to steal from, murder, and generally take advantage of their fellow man".

"The theory is, Becky," interjected Willy, "that people would be less like to be villainous if they knew that they would probably meet their victims in the afterlife, in Annwn, and that they would very definitely have to pay for their actions through the interaction of the immutable Law of Karma, and that that penance might take a lot longer than just one lifetime. Think about how long Hitler and Pol Pot might have to do penance, not that I have a clue either, but it has to be quite a while.

"Think about it. Nobody would mug old ladies, if they thought that there was no escape - guaranteed no escape from being out and being punished!"

"Crime would be slashed in days, if this were taught in schools".

"Why isn't it then, Dad?"

"Vested interest, Becky", said her mother. "The established churches don't want to lose their power. They and the governing class work together to maintain the status quo. The problem with the real teachings is that they are quite revolutionary - certainly in some senses of the word. They don't preach violence, but Mahatma Gandhi showed how to circumvent that problem, which was why he was assassinated, and there have been many like him though far less famous outside their own spheres of influence.

"Therefore, the goal of proving life after death is to better the lot of mankind, which would cause a more equitable distribution of resources, which would allow people to spend more time on their Spiritual Development…"

"…and less time on slaving for a pittance", added her father.

"Have you both become revolutionaries? Well, I always knew that Dad was one, but not you Mam".

"It's not that, love. The system in force in most of the world encourages greed, which depends on subjugation, and that is wrong. I don't advocate overthrowing or killing anyone, I want them to realise that the current way is not the way forward. It is not even a way forward. Given rising populations, the current economic system will and can only lead to more of the same or worse.

"There are greedy people in charge who have more money than their families will ever be able to spend in generations, yet still they are not satisfied. They want more. These people are sick, they should not be in charge, but in the World, they are revered and held up as examples of intelligence and hard work. However, you can't look to the North, South or East for good examples either. The correct philosophy is there, but again, it has been corrupted by greedy people.

"The only answer is Spiritual Knowledge, which means education, and since schools will never be allowed to teach it, because the curriculum is controlled by the greedy and modelled to produce obedient workers, not thinking Good Samaritans, it is up go us and like-minded people on The Surface to show people the correct Path".

"The Middle Way…" said Becky quietly. "Hatha and Raja Yoga".

"Yes. Yoga and the correct thought that it encourages, is one of the best first steps in that direction, and, just for your information, Yoga classes are banned from many church halls that are thrown open to other public learning activities".

"I didn't know that", said Becky, "but I can see why they might be now. Who'd have thought that Yoga could lead to the stealthy revolution?"

"Some people have identified it as a big enough threat to ban it. Do your own research".

"All right, so what do we do? How do we go about this?"

"There are only two ways basically", said Sarah. "Established churches are not likely to let you use their halls, so, you either have to build a Sanctuary, or buy and refurbish an abandoned church like Gareth and Emma's group did".

"I suppose you could join them for a while, if you like, and then start out alone when you have more confidence, couldn't she, Mam?"

"Yes, that would be fine. In fact, whatever you decide to do is fine. Even if you don't want to do anything at all. It is completely your decision. So, having dropped that bombshell on you, we will leave now to let you think it over".

"But I wanted to tell Becky about our holiday!"

"Yes, well, it'll keep. Bye for now, Becky, go with God". Willy waved and they both vanished, leaving Becky wondering what to do next, so she made a cup of tea.

10 MEETING OLD FRIENDS

"How do you think the lesson went with Becky tonight, love?" asked Willy.

"Oh, very well, think, much the same as ever, but we did leave her with a great deal to think about".

"Yes, that's what I meant really. Do you think she'll go for it? I mean, it would mean a considerable amount of extra work for her - and possibly John and the boys?".

"I think that she will do it, but all we can do is set up opportunities and hope that some of them are taken up. If Becky is not ready yet, then we just look around for someone else, and whether we look hard or not or wait for her is immaterial. It is our job, as I see it, to keep trying to advance the cause of Spirit, because Spirit is completely selfless, so if that is advanced then other issues will rise on the tide with it... including humanity".

"Do you know what I think is strange?" he said staring into the fire in their hearth, "I can't understand why she hasn't come up here to visit us".

"Yes. Who knows. Perhaps, she doesn't want to intrude now that we are together again".

"Could be, I suppose. She used to pop in quite often when I was here on my own".

"Well, I'm not surprised about that! You weren't looking after yourself, the dog or the cottage! Least not until you came back from Annwn. That visit changed your life around, didn't it?"

"Yes, it did. It made me realise that there is no point in giving up, if life is going to continue anyway".

"And that is exactly the point that I was making to Becky this evening! If people realised that there was a continuation after this life on

Life in Annwn

The Surface, then they wouldn't be so rotten to one another".

"Yes, I vet your argument, and I agree with you. Most thefts are opportunistic in nature because they think that they unobserved, but if they knew for a guaranteed fact that they would have to pay for every misdemeanour because everything is being recorded and you will punish yourself for any crime anyway, people would see the futility in behaving badly.

" Then we wouldn't need such a large police force or army, and that extra labour could be productive instead of er, not, I suppose".

"It would allow a complete overhaul of society if there were less crime and no greediness."

"We wouldn't need Trident or any weapons or the forces that use them. Think of the savings that would bring about!"

"Yes. It's but a dream at the moment, but it will come, and the Spirit World is the only place that the movement can originate from. Think about that.

"Tomorrow, after we've checked the two new puppies, I'd like you to come with me to meet some people. Are you up for that yet?"

"Oh, I don't know. I don't really want to, but if you want me to I will. Do I know them, or did I?"

"Some of them, yes. They're nice. You'll like them".

"OK", he said warily, "if you say so".

∞

They took themselves to the city of Annwn and to the main square, where they politely passed the time of day with the landlord of the inn and then walked on.

"We're going in here", said Sarah suddenly, and led Willy through the open door into a spacious, 1920's art-deco coffee shop with dozens of seating areas that were all partially secluded, and all slightly different. Strategically-placed potted plants and palms made it easy to hold fairly private conversations and discussions.

"They usually sit around the back here somewhere", she said easily over the soft jazz music which provided further privacy. "Yes, here we are. Ready? Good. Here we go.

"Hello, everyone! You all remember my husband, William, better known to all and sundry as Willy. I'll do the introductions later, if their names don't come back to you, Willy, but I always find that lengthy initial lengthy introductions almost always get forgotten, don't you?"

"Yes, it's one of our sillier social customs", said one middle-aged man dressed in jeans and a 'V-necked' sweater. Come and sit by me, there's plenty of room for two more".

Sarah led the way over. "Do these people all know that they're dead?" asked Willy.

Sarah laughed. "Willy is asking whether you all know that you're dead!" she chuckled. "The only other group he's met were old soldiers - they didn't".

"Yes, we are all quite aware of what is going on, Willy. My name is Matthew. Mat for short. Do you remember me? We have all been coming in here every afternoon for as long as I can remember. We often hold fascinating debates on important issues, and you were always up for a good discussion!"

"No, Mat, sorry. Have we met before?"

"Oh, you're still suffering from Surface Block, are you? Yes, we've been friends for a very long time… since long before you went back this time. How long has Willy been back now, Sarah?"

"Oh, five or six Surface months?"

"Oh, not so long really. It can take years to get rid of the Block. Never mind. Trust Sarah and your other friends and you will work your way through it eventually. You know that it's induced before you are reborn so that you don't remember what you planned to do on The Surface, but it does last some time after coming back too… It's different each trip and for each person, but it does always recede. Always, so don't worry about it.

"Allow me to order you a drink. What are you having?"

Life in Annwn

Willy looked around the table and saw that black coffee seemed to be the in-drink. "Is that a black coffee?" he said pointing at Mat's half-empty cup.

"Yes. I can recommend it with Tia Maria".

"That sounds great to me. Sarah?" She nodded assent. "Two, please, Mat".

"I'll do the honours, Mat!" said a voice from the far end of the table.

"Thanks, Roger.

"Where were we... Oh, yes the Block. It's the main reason why loved ones on The Surface find it disappointing that their departed loved ones haven't returned to tell them about the Afterlife. They don't realise that those who recently passed over just don't remember how to do it any longer. They have to relearn how to go back!

"And if that can take years, they end up drawing the wrong conclusion... either that the person doesn't care, or that there is no Afterlife. It's a real problem and a real shame too".

"Sometimes, it's possible for a friend to go back and explain", said a woman in her Twenties, who was dressed as a flapper, complete with beads and a feather in her hair. Willy looked at Sarah and pointed at the woman with his chin as surreptitiously as he could. Sarah smiled back.

"Willy is admiring your get-up, Joy. It's perfect, isn't it, Willy?"

"Er, yes, that's exactly what I was thinking".

"Oh, thank you dwarling. I do try - not like some I could mention. It's not all doom and gloom, is it? You have to balance that with some fun. Anyway, Willy, I'm Joy. I was just listening to your conversation with Mat. You probably don't remember me either then, but you will! You used to dress up to.

"I thought you would have become an actor when you returned to The Surface, but Sarah said that you were a shepherd! No wonder you've come back so quiet, dwarling. What was that like?"

"I loved it, Joy - nice to meet you again", he said holding a hand up because the table was a little too wide to stretch across. It was very peaceful... it gave me a lot of time to think, and just be with the animals and nature".

"It sounds divine, dwarling. You didn't have to fend off wolves or poachers then?"

"No", he chuckled, "no wolves... not in Wales... not any more, but you never knew when someone might try to shoot one for an easy few bucks".

"So it was tewibly dangerous then?"

"No, I wouldn't say so, would you, Sarah?"

"Oh, I'm sure that I wouldn't know. I was only a housewife, but you were always a hero to me", she said and drew his shoulder to hers. Willy could tell that something was going on, but wasn't sure what.

"Do you still like jazz music, Willy?" asked Roger from down the table.

"Er, yes, although I don't remember ever listening to it on our mountain. We certainly didn't buy any, did we, Sarah"

"No, I don't think so, love".

"S'funny, you used to be such a fan before. What did you use to listen to on your mountain?"

He looked at Sarah before answering. "Well, I was outside most of the time, but when I could, on a Sunday, like, I would play choirs... mostly Welsh Male-Voice, and brass band music, especially Colliery Brass Bands. I found them stirring and very poignant".

"Oh, I'm sure they are... we all like jazz - you used to too".

"Did I? All those years alone with the sheep must have done something to me", he answered with a smile. "I like this music though. I like it a lot.

"Could I ask a general question, please?" he said across the table. "Have any of you lived on The Surface since we last met, or are Sarah and I the only ones?" They looked around the table at one another and a few mumbled chats took place, the Roger said,

"Well, I haven't, and I don't think that any of you have either, have you?" he asked looking at the faces around the table. Heads were being shaken and and scratched. "No, come to think of it, none of us has been back for quite a while. Why do you ask?"

"I don't rightly know to be honest, but my life, er, my experience on The Surface has changed me, hasn't it? I feel that it probably has anyway, since I used to be a part of this group, yes?"

"And still are, old boy! You still are!" said a rich-looking gent in an evening suit with tails, a why shirt with butterfly-collars and a dicky bow. Willy wondered whether he was Joy's partner.

"Thank you. I am happy here. It has nothing to do with that. I love the decor and the music… and you all have been very friendly to me. It's just that, if I used to sit here every afternoon, I probably couldn't any more. Once in a while - great, but not every day… not any more. No offence, but we enjoy helping lonely puppies now, and we're hoping to set up a church with our daughter on The Surface. We want to spread the word about life after death and reincarnation to help rid the World of starvation and war".

"Ah! Yes… very worthwhile goals, that's for sure. We have debated the topic many, many times - you were one of its strongest proponents. It was your hobby-horse, you could say. You always won the day with the strength of your argument and commitment. My word, yes.

"Today's debate was proposed by Jeremy. It is entitled, "Is the Aristocracy still fulfilling a worthwhile function in European Society?' I am sure that that topic will produce a lively discussion. We know that it usually does".

"However, I am certain that I speak for every man and woman here, when I say that we wish you the very best in your quest. You will always find us here right behind you in your endeavours. Isn't that correct, fellow members of the Inner City Jazz Club?"

Everybody nodded, said 'Aye', tapped the table or expressed unison in their own way.

"Well, that's really nice to know… isn't it, Sarah?"

"Yes, darling", she replied with a smile in her eyes.

Two coffees and liqueurs later, they shook hands with or kissed all those there present and left and as they were walking away, they could here Roger calling the group to order to discuss the motion of the day.

"And they do that every day?" asked William.

"Yes, pretty much. Not everyone turns up absolutely every day, though a few do".

"Roger - I suppose…"

"Yes".

"Did I too?"

"I used to go there quite often, and one day you said that you were interested in the title of the next day's debate. You attended that one and quite regularly after that, until you went up to The Surface. You were one of the best debaters in the group".

"Did I only use to go to be near you?"

"I used to hope so…"

"Probably… although they do seem a nice bunch".

"Oh, yes, if ever you weren't sure how to spell a word, they would rather tell you than have a member who can't spell".

"Is that a little harsh?"

"Perhaps, but they don't actually do much except debate. You opened my eyes to that… "

"Is that why we went to The Surface together?"

"Yes… You showed me that words are fine, and absolutely necessary in order to establish policy, but sooner or later, action is needed".

"So, we decided to go to The Surface to take action… but what did we achieve? I became a shepherd and you a housewife".

"I don't know, my dear, but we had a daughter, and we don't know what she will achieve; and the two of us have learned a lot, and are prepared to take action. I suppose that you were before, but you have recruited me, and we have recruited Becky. Not only that, but you showed thousands of people in the village and in the prison that not only are there kind people in the world, but that performing kind acts actually makes one feel better.

" All that must have advanced the cause. The Universe is in a better predicament now than before we were reborn, and none of that would have been accomplished, if we had remained in the Inner City Jazz Club, would it?" He reached over and kissed her on her temple.

"I love you, dwarling!

"You have a wonderful way of putting everything into perspective. There is no-one that I would prefer to spend my time with than you".

"You don't really know anyone else!"

"Well, no, I suppose I don't, but if I did, I would still choose you. The way you stuck by me on our mountain, and the way you are still doing it mow, means a great deal to me. It really does".

"Thank you, my dear".

"I know why I stay with you, but, er, why do you stay with me, if you don't mind me asking?"

"I stay with you because I love you, and because you inspire me. I want to make a difference. I thought I was before, but you made me realise that there was more. I had been born on The Surface before, but I was a bit like the others back there… I thought that once was enough. Life here is easy, on The Surface, it wasn't… I didn't want to go through that again, but you showed me that it was the easiest way for a person to make a difference.

"I was dubious at first, but you were right. It is as plain as the nose on your face now, but I didn't know that then. Or maybe I did, but I didn't fancy the discomfort of Surface life. It is easier when you go with someone… although it wasn't just that with me. I did, and still do, love you, Willy".

"And you are my rock, Sarah, and I love you very much too".

"Thank you, my dear. Let's go home to our little cottage and our mountain".

Moments later, they were sitting in their respective armchairs before a roaring fire even though it was impossible for them to feel temperature. The real flames were as fascinating for them as they were when they were incorporate. They held hands as Willy stared into the glow.

"I really hope that Becky wants to set up the church. What do you think, my dear?"

"Well, I am quietly confident that she will, and I will tell you why. She is our daughter.

"I know that that is a trite saying, but there is some truth in it. You have probably not remembered yet, my dear, but, we can go over that again sometime. Basically, Becky chose to be born to us, and we accepted her. So, why would she have chosen us, if our basic philosophies were at odds?

"She wouldn't have, and we wouldn't have accepted her either for the same reason. Therefore, I am certain that Becky will go with it. She might be scared or shy or something, I am certain that she will be. She is here to learn through challenges too, like all of us, but deep down, she will want this.

"I would not be surprised if we have to encourage her, but if we handle that

that well, and give her all the support she needs, she will do it… or I'm a monkey's uncle!"

"And I for one believe you, dwarling. Should we get in touch with her?"

"I wouldn't. The agreement is that she will confirm our meeting the day before, as usual, and, if we don't see her before that, we can ask her then. Remember that we talked about building a Sanctuary, or buying an abandoned church? Well, what is wrong with having it here?"

"In our home?"

"Well, yes, but it's not as if we need a home, is it? And there won't be people running around the place all day and all night, will there? This is the ideal place for a Sanctuary, and it has already been paid for, so, Becky can't use expense as a bulwark".

"You are a crafty one, Sarah Jones. I wouldn't like to play chess with you!"

Life in Annwn

11 FAMILY

"You said something the other day that intrigued me", said Willy one evening in front of the fire.

"Really? Only once in several days? Either I must be slipping or your memory must be returning".

"No, nothing like that", he chortled enjoying his wife's sense of humour, something that he hadn't noticed when they had been in corporate. "You said that you were pretty certain that Becky would go for the church idea - and you were right - but, why did you say that we wouldn't have all ended up together, if she hadn't been amenable to the idea in the first place?"

"Yes, this subject has been on the agenda for a while, it is quite central to our way of life. As we have said before, life as we know it is but a university, and the goal is knowledge in all its guises including experience. We can then use this knowledge and experience to help others, which also helps ourselves through the action of Karma. Helping others actually is helping ourselves and is the only way that Spirit can achieve satisfaction and development. It is imperative to 'help forward', as they call it now. Returning a favour carries less weight, but is better than nothing.

"So, once that fact has been established, life becomes a quest for knowledge. It is possible to learn things here in Annwn, but in reality, Annwn is like a theoretic bubble. For example, you can learn about poverty here, but you cannot experience it, since real poverty can lead to hunger, sickness and the early death of one's loved ones, which cannot happen here because we do not need food and do not procreate.

"This is Paradise, where no harm can befall you, so there are many 'real life situations' that we cannot experience here. We have to go to The

Surface, or one of the infinite number of other places, schools or universities, if you like, to do that".

"So, what sort of level school is Earth on?"

"I am not exactly certain, but from my research, I think that it's roughly equivalent to a junior school".

"What! Not even a lower university?"

"No, afraid not, not even a technical college, but that shouldn't disappoint you... leastwise, it doesn't me. It means that I am at the start of my journey, not near its end, and I find that tremendously exciting.

"Who knows how much further there is to travel and what wonders there are to behold?"

"And the journey lasts forever?"

""Yes, as far as I know. We are so far down the scale that that we can only see so far ahead, and can only comprehend so much of what we see, even from here. We are a few feet off sea-level up a mountain, the vast bulk of which is shrouded in clouds above us. I know that you enjoyed Star Trek as a kid, but the top of that mountain is the real Final Frontier, not space, which, like Earth or The Surface, or any other 'place', does not exist outside of our imagination.

"Sorry, Sarah, I can follow that, but how does it tie Becky in with us?"

"Remember when we first started thinking about Becky going to university?"

"Yes, we had to look for accommodation in Cardiff and..."

"Yes, but, wait a minute. That was not the beginning of the story. It didn't start there". She took a moment's pause so that Willy could think about it.

"Becky didn't actually go to university until she was eighteen, but the journey started when she was fourteen. Remember? She came home from school one day with a list of classes that she could choose from, but some of those classes overlapped so she couldn't do both?"

"Yes... I remember that she had to give up Welsh and Latin, if she wanted to do the sciences".

"Exactly, so she had to think of a career, or at least a general area of interest, and choose the subjects that would allow her to enter that field".

"Yes, sure, and then the same happened again two years later".

"Yes, she had to further refine her interests and choose three subjects to match. She wanted to go into Social Services, so she chose English, History and Welsh".

"Then, before she could go to take up her studies, she had to choose the best one that she could qualify to go to…right?" Willy nodded, getting into the swing of it now, "Then, she had to go for interviews, and wait for her exam results. Yes?".

"Yes…"

"And it was only then, that we had to find digs for her. There were four years of activity before she walked through the first university classroom door. Four years!

"Well, it's a lot like that in life. It's not just a big surprise when you pop out of your mother's womb, even though it takes nine months to grow a viable body for a Soul to inhabit. Let's say that you want to have a particular experience. We'll keep it simple for now and just talk about one experience, even though a person goes through thousands of them in a life in corporate. Say, that you wanted to experience life as a poor man, because there are things that a poor man can learn that a rich man never would, and vice versa, of course.

"You would need to be born into a poor family, wouldn't you?"

"Yes, that makes sense…"

"Well, you're not going to learn it in a rich family. However, you could add a twist. You could choose a rich family that loses all it's money. Do you want to add discrimination to mix? Religious, colour, weight, disability… which one or ones?

"So, how many rich families are there, which have decided that they are going to lose all their money? Then, if you want colour discrimination, it will need to be of which colour and in which country? Do you want to add a disability? Then you will have to find a rich couple of colour that had already planned to lose all its money, who are willing to share the experience of having a disabled child.

Life in Annwn

"You can already see how it can become very complicated. And the more you add in, the more complex it becomes to find the right woman to be born to. This can take lengthy negotiations or interviews. One day, you will find the right hosts, or family, or, you could plan it even further in advance and arrange your future parents here before even they are born! Some people put a great deal into their planning, others less so.

"So, the big day comes and you get into the driving seat of your new body. That involves invoking the Block, which is meant to obscure your memories of Life Before Birth. It is interesting that sometimes the Block is not one hundred percent effective, and that some people obtain special dispensation to be born without the Block.

"Then, at birth, you could say that the student has walked though the classroom door. It is usually a very long process, and is not undertaken lightly... in fact, I have never met anyone who just did it 'for a laugh'.

"Why would the parents want to involve themselves with anyone so frivolous? It doesn't happen. However, things can go wrong. The foetus may have been meant to develop perfectly, but doesn't. The brain's wiring can be faulty... there are many things that can happen unplanned, while other abnormalities have been planned. It's just one of those things, not all machines are perfect, especially not biological ones.

"So, some people had planned to have a perfect body, but don't get one. It happens. Other times, people get the life they intended, but it is too difficult for them. They have overreached themselves, if you like. The 'students' in both of these latter categories can decide to drop out, which, in Surface terms, means commit suicide.

"This is catastrophic, a total tragedy, for all the family concerned, not least because of all the effort that had been put into the placing of that soul in the correct environment - or in the correct class at university.

"Everyone loses! It is not the loss of life, it is the wasted effort in planning and the potential effect of that life on others".

"But the Block prevents them from seeing all that, eh?"

"Yes, although an act of suicide is often the result of temporary weakness... all that planning and work by many people ruined in a moment".

"The Church decries suicide too, but for slightly the wrong reason. I seem to be coming across that quite often. It's as if it's doing the right thing, but for the wrong reasons… some of the times, anyway… as if it has become distorted".

"Yes, whether by imperfect translations or copiers, or deliberate falsification… it has happened".

"Are you planning to be reborn soon, Sarah?"

"No, not really, although it is always in the back of my mind - a bit like holidays. How about you?" She felt a little hurt that he should ask so soon after re-establishing their relationship. At least, she thought that that was what they had done.

"No, not at all! I still don't know what's going on! I don't know what I would have done if it hadn't been for you".

"Ach, someone else would have come to your assistance. No-one is indispensable".

"Perhaps not, but I am glad that it was you… is you, by my side. So, we were friends here first, and then we chose to go to The Surface together to carry on".

"Not to 'carry on', We were married".

"Pardon?" he asked not getting her joke straight away. "Yes, very quick… 'continue' then".

"Yes, but marriage is not a piece of paper in Annwn. We didn't make any plans for after being on The Surface. I mean for when we were both back here, so we are both free agents again". It was Willy's turn to feel hurt.

"Did you get everything out of being on our mountain that you had hoped for?"

"Yes, I have no complaints. How about you?"

"Definitely no complaints, but I don't remember what I was there for. Did I tell you?"

"We discussed it like I just said. Being reborn involves many discussions with many people".

"And one of those was Becky, eh?"

"Yes. Becky was in on the trip from very early on. We met her before we were reborn".

"I see. So, we were some of those long-term planners you were just telling me about".

"Yes. Ours was not that complex, but it did go further than a lot of people do. Our rebirths were not 'solo projects', as they are often called, not that anything like that could ever be achieved on one's own. Think about it! How could anyone be reborn alone? It takes two parents and another. Life itself depends upon cooperation - it cannot take place without cooperation, and it certainly cannot continue in isolation… yet some people on The Surface seem to think that it can, or they lead their lives as if no-one else matters anyway".

"In splendid isolation…"

"I don't know how isolation can be splendid… It's used as a punishment in prisons, people very rarely laugh out loud when alone, and it is definitely easier to have fun when not alone". He scrutinised her face in order to judge whether she was making a saucy joke, but she kept a straight face.

"Yes, all of that is true. Loners and strangers never look as if they are having much fun. Was I a loner on the mountain?"

"No, not really… Your job involved being alone, but you loved to go to the pub for a chin-wag with your mates as well".

"Yes, but I enjoyed my job too".

"All p art of the planning, I guess".

"If you so, my dear".

"You were not and are not a miserable person, Willy. Serious, yes, but miserable, no, and there's nothing wrong with that. You always struck me as a man with a mission", she said smiling.

"You make me sound like Action Man", he said joking. "Me, a lowly shepherd…"

"It has happened before", she replied enigmatically.

"Oh, oh, yes, so it has!" he laughed embarrassed. "A different league though".

"Perhaps, but all Spirit is moving in the same direction... we are all progressing towards the same goal and we are all working together... In fact, it is the only way to achieve our end".

"The Spirit of Co-operation..."

"Yes, I like that. The Spirit of Co-operation - very good. We could call our Sanctuary that".

"This place?"

"Yes, why not?"

"No, reason, OK. So, Becky has been part of our team for longer than she has been our daughter, and it is, therefore, very unlikely that she will not go for the concept".

"Yes, 'though she may 'Um' and 'Ah' a bit because of the Block, but she will come around eventually. You'll see".

"That's good enough for me, Sarah".

"Let's invite her over".

∞

Becky parked her car opposite her old birthplace and sat looking at the tired old house for a few minutes. She had had a sudden urge to visit the old place. John wanted to sell it, but she was loathe to part with it. There was too much history... too much of her very being tied up in it. If they were going to keep it, they would have to put some work into though. It looked as if the very house itself were dying since her father had passed on. All the external woodwork needed repainting, and the rough, unpainted boards that had been used for temporary shuttering over the windows was looking worse than anything. The weeds and even the plants belied the fact that the garden was being neglected.

Most properly developers would put a ball and chain through it, she thought, and got out of the car. The latch on the gate had rusted solid, so she took her shoe off to hit it with until it gave way and creaked open.. she was dreading going inside, but something was driving her to take a look. As soon as she opened the front door, she was struck by the musty smell and the dingy interior. She was about to put a light on to find her way around, when she noticed that it wasn't cold, which surprised her since it was October.

Willy and Sarah had been aware of her since her arrival and were watching her.

"Becky", said her mother, "welcome home. Sit down, dear, your father and I would like to have a talk". Becky didn't quite hear the words, but pulled out a stool from the corner and sat down.

"Mam, Dad, are you here?".

"Yes", said Sarah, as they resumed their seats. "Can you hear me now?"

"Yes, Mam, and I can see you both. Something made me want to come here today, well, last night really, but it was too late. I wasn't expecting to see you here though. It's just like old times".

12 THE SPIRIT OF CO-OPERATION

Becky sat on the stool by the fire as she had thousands of times as a child. She was looking around herself waiting for her parents to speak. She couldn't help noticing the dust and cobwebs, things that her mother would never have allowed when she was alive. She wondered whether she could see them now, whether she cared or not, and whether she could actually do anything about them even if she did.

The fact was that her parents couldn't see them, although Sarah could have if she tried, but the dust and cobwebs were on a different vibration, which made them difficult for Willy and her to see, and they chose not to see the boarding, so the house looked clean and cosy to them.

In a similar way, Becky couldn't see the blazing fire in the grate, although she was vaguely aware of its heat. It wasn't roasting hot, as it might have been if it was a Surface fire, but she an emanation from the hearth that she perceived as warmth.

"Did you hear your mother speaking to you yesterday, Becky?"

"I was vaguely aware of you, Mam, but I can't say that I heard you. No, but I did have an overwhelming compulsion to come up here, whereas I've only set foot in the place twice since, er, you know…"

"Don't worry about it. It's probably the distance. Your power of reception will improve with use and confidence. You know we are here, so it is not difficult to believe that we are talking to you, but to just hear my voice out of the blue while you are doing the washing up, well, that's something else. That's to be expected".

"Are you living here permanently now?"

"Permanent" is a difficult word for us, darling, but we do have plans for the cottage, and, yes, they do involve you, if you are interested".

"Before I passed on, Becky, you might remember that we talked of perhaps trying to set up something like Gareth and Emma have bus with your mother as our contact".

"Yes, sort of… Sometimes, I think that I've forgotten a great deal from those days".

"Never mind, I imagine that it will come back to you. Well, it seems that that is something that your mother has wanted for some time, and that that isn't a coincidence".

"What do you think of the idea now, Becky?" asked Sarah.

"I wouldn't know how to go about it… I don't even know if I have the time or the ability…"

"What if I said that you do?"

"I would say, 'Thank you, Mam, you have always encouraged me, but I would be sceptical".

"OK. Do you have any plans for this cottage?"

"No, not really. I don't want to sell it, but John is talking about it. He wants a new car and says that the family deserves a holiday".

"We were thinking that it would be perfect for a Sanctuary - like Gareth's converted church. Imagine it! It is secluded and quiet, and has a wonderfully warm atmosphere. The location, near the top of a mountain, is ideal too. The air is clean and pure, and the stars so close that you feel you could reach up and touch them. That would be perfect for outdoor meditation".

"Yes, I can see that, Mam, but the old place is a bit, er, well, ramshackle, isn't it? It would need to be restored".

"Yes. You are probably right, but not too much. It has character and ambiance - we wouldn't want to lose that".

"Well, that's another thing, isn't it? Finance. Where would we get the money from to do any work on the place, if we are not going to sell it? John reckoned that we could borrow ten thousand on it, do it up and sell it for seventy or eighty, but the bank probably wouldn't do that if we were going to turn it into a church".

"Don't worry about the money", said Sarah. "The first job is to get the ideas right. Once we have agreed on that, then we can think about the finances".

"And what about John?"

"Leave him to us. What about you?"

"Count me in, Mam, I never wanted to sell our old home anyway. Are you living in it?"

"We rest here, you could call that living here, but we don't have any possessions, and we could still stay here, even if another family moved in".

"Wouldn't that be like haunting the place?"

"Yes, but millions of places are 'haunted', if you want to define it like that, but the people who live there are unaware of their co-habitants, because they don't have the ability to see them, or rather the knowledge to look for them. That wouldn't bother us, and probably not them either. You don't think that every so-called ghost that walks the Earth has been spotted, do you? They, we are everywhere… as commonplace as cats and dogs in a city!"

"I didn't realise…"

"No, most people don't, but it's true, nevertheless. So, are we on?" asked Sarah.

Becky looked around at the dusty ceiling, the long-unpainted rafters and other woodwork, the threadbare carpet and the ugly shuttering covering the ancient windows and nodded. Almost imperceptibly at first, but then more forcefully. "Yes. This is our house, not John's, and if you still have a use for it, then it's all yours. Do you really think that we can make a go of it?"

"Yes, Becky, I am. The need is there, and the three of us have the ability to fulfil it, so what can go wrong? We are doing it for the right reasons - for the good of the community, certainly not for ours, and not even for yours, as it will involve considerable effort on your behalf and no financial reward".

"John will be pleased", said Becky sarcastically. "He has been dropping massive hints that it's time I found another job for the last few weeks now".

"It's funny," interjected Willy, "but if you look at this scenario from a certain angle, Mam's passing, and then mine, and your losing your job because of it, all those things are the very things that make this project possible. It's almost as if it had been planned!"

Sarah looked at him and smiled, "Well, I don't believe in coincidence". Becky was not party to the private joke, but what her mother said gave her food for thought.

"Er, I don't know how to say this, Mam, but are you aware how grotty this place looks?"

"I haven't looked, my dear. To us, it is surface dirt, and since we can't interact with anything physically dense, it doesn't affect us, but don't worry about it. It will all be spotlessly clean when the restoration work has been completed".

"What about the shutters on the windows? They are so awful! Shall I have them removed as soon as possible?"

"No, my dear, not before work starts. They don't bother us, leave them. Well, shall we call it a day there, and let you get back to your family, Becky. Just think about what we have discussed, and know that if your heart is in the project, then nothing can go wrong, because Spirit is working from this side to ensure it's success".

"OK, I will go home, via the shops, but I will give this a lot of thought. We will probably meet again at our weekly class. Good night, both, I love you".

"Good night, Becky, go with God!" said her mother.

"Bye, cariad", said her father.

"How do you fancy going out for a bit?"

"OK, where do you have in mind?"

"Well, there's someone I'd like to see, now that we have Becky's go-ahead. Wait a sec, I'll see whether they are available". Sarah closed her eyes and appeared to go to sleep in her chair. He didn't like to stare while her attention was elsewhere, so he just gazed into the flames of the fire - something that he had always enjoyed doing since he was a child.

"Julia said that she can see us now, if we are ready. Are you?" she asked.

"Yes, my dear. Whenever you are".

"Good. We need to go into the Learning Centre in Annwn. Just wish yourself to be standing outside it before the main entrance. They were both instantly there. "Right, we want Room 46. Same principle. See you outside it on the staircase. Go!

"You are doing extremely well. Now, we are going in to see a senior Guide called Julia. Julia has many contacts and a huge amount of experience, so we are here to pick her brains about setting up our new 'Spirit of Co-operation. After you," she said.

Willy gave her a look of might be called mild trepidation, and pushed the open door inwards. Sarah followed him in. As on the previous occasions, they were standing alone in a large oblong room, which had windows along two of its curved, stone walls. It was ridiculously large for the tower that it was in and the scenery through the windows was blurry and nondescript being basically blue at the top and green along the bottom.

"Julia!" said Sarah softly, but still loud enough to surprise him. Her voice resonated in the excellent acoustics of the room. Suddenly, a tall, smiling woman of about thirty was walking towards them from a few feet away. She was performing the Buddhist waai greeting of holding her two hands flat together before her chin.

Sarah did the same in return and Willy copied her. "Hello, Julia! This is Willy, my very old friend from The Surface and here before that". They nodded and smiled at one another. "We just talked to another friend, who was our Surface daughter, and want to establish a Learning Centre in our old home on a mountain in South Wales. We have the building and the land, so all we need now is help and finance.

"This is our first one. It's very exciting".

"Yes. I remember that we talked about it before you were reborn onto The Surface. Why don't you take a seat, while I reacquaint myself with the details?" Sarah and Willy sat at a couch by a coffee table and Julia sat opposite them. "OK. You have quite a lot of friends in the area, haven't you? And there are many who remember Willy from the prison visiting scheme. Yes, you have a very strong base to build on. This visit looks as if it was extremely well planned…"

Sarah looked at Willy proudly, "That was mostly your doing", she said to his surprise.

"Congratulations are in order then. Anyway, as I said, there is or will be a lot of ground-swell sympathy for this project, if your daughter recruits the right help and they put some effort into spreading the word about what you intend to do.

"I am confident that the right people will step forward to help, but if they are a tad slow, come back and see me and we will consider a more direct approach. Start by announcing your intentions in the local paper and ask for Founder Members to contact you.

"Is there anything else I can help you with?"

"Willy?"

He shook his head rather dumbfounded, but managed, "No, Julia, thank you for the encouragement".

"No, nor have I", continued Sarah standing up. "Thanks, Julia. It was lovely to see you again".

"Yes. Keep me informed of your progress. I don't foresee any problems with this one. Your farming friends will help, and there's a builder not far away who is becoming increasingly interested in the Afterlife, as he calls it, since his mother returned to Annwn recently. If you ask me, I will put her on to you. I'm sure that she would love to help.

"Bye for now, both". Willy was already halfway towards the door, but when he turned to respond, Julia had vanished and Sarah was approaching him quickly.

"Well, that went well, didn't it?"

"Yes, it's far easier to get planning permission here than on The Surface… and funding". He noticed that he had called it The Surface… perhaps for the first time since he had been back in Annwn. "Where now?" he asked.

"Home?" she answered, and they were both back in their armchairs before the fire, which never seemed to die down.

"Is there anything else you want to do right at this moment, or shall we get on with the 'The Spirit'?" she asked keen to press on with a project that was more than a hundred Surface years in the planning and now approaching a phase where actual physical activity was imminent. Sarah's elevated mood did not escape him and he did not want to disappoint her.

"Oh, we have to ride the wave and go with the flow, my dear, but it is all a little above my head at the moment. I know that you credited me with having initiated and organized the scheme at the outset, but I don't remember that and. To be honest, I am feeling a little out of my depth".

"Don't worry about hour memory, that will return sooner or later. Let's stick with this for now then… Maybe, it will jolt your mind to raise The Block".

"Let's hope so. Where do we go from here?"

"That is up to us. This is our project, but as with everything, there is always someone ready to help, if we need it. I suggest that we formulate an idea of what we want this place to look like, and for that, we need to think about what we want to achieve here, and then we present that to Becky, and let her tackle the problems as she sees fit, with us in the background always ready to give advice and support, just as we always have Julia ready to help and support us"

"I can see that it is better not to try to run the whole show from here, because there are physical things that need to be done that we are not capable of doing… we can't place an ad in a newspaper or put one brick on top of another for example, can we?"

"No, we need human assistance, but we can advise, encourage and support. They are our roles. The actual physical implementation has to be theirs… However, that is good, because it means that they retain a lot of control and that encourages participation, which is precisely what we need".

"We boost their egos, and they do our bidding", he remarked.

"Oh, I think that that's a very unkind way of expressing the

Life in Annwn

mechanics of how it works!"

"That's how it would be expressed on The Surface!"

"By cynics, perhaps…"

"If Surface Dwellers were using our tactics to achieve their ends, that is how it could be described".

"All right. I don't agree with you, I don't intend brushing up anyone's ego, but let's say that that is so for the purpose of this discussion. We are not doing this for our own good, but for the good of people who are ruining their future by building up bad Karma while on The Surface because they do not understand what they are doing".

"Yes, OK. I'll go along with that too. So, what next?"

"Next is to decide what we want to achieve with the 'Spirit of Co-operation'. It was your concept, so let's discuss that. Can you remember anything at all about what you wanted to do?"

"No, not really, although I can see that it would be good to enlighten people about their Karma, so that they don't blight their own near future. It seems to me that that would be the best service we could offer our friends and family in the local community where we lived all of our lives".

"I wonder if we have spent other lives here…" she said.

"Pardon?"

"Oh, it was just that you said 'all of our lives'. I know that you were referring to the whole of both of our last life on The Surface, but it could also be interpreted as literally 'all our lives'. Well, we have all had many lives, I was just wondering how many of them we have spent here on this mountain".

"Oh, I see… Well, there was that teacher, I think he was, who lives in Cheddar Gorge, and he shares DNA with one of the skeletons found in the caves. So, that means that his family hasn't moved from that village for 20,000 years! I suppose the same could be true of us, we'd have to find some old bones first and get Becky to go and compare her DNA… Mmm, it is interesting".

"Yes, but we're getting off track. Let's try to focus!"

'Crikey, you started it!' he thought.

"Yes, and I'm I did. I wish I'd kept it back for later, but let's do try to get on".

They talked about the new Sanctuary until they were both too emotionally drained to continue and had to stop for the time being.

"I think that we've hammered out the basis of a good building that will suit our needs admirably", opined Willy. "I can't really see it costing a fortune either".

"No, the most expensive part will be the new annex on the back, but that is really only for 'other purposes', and since we don't have any members yet, there is no real need for it yet either".

"No, that's right. It can be what they call in the building industry, a ' hospital job', meaning that they can take their time over it, which means less cost, but longer to wait. What about all of our stuff in here and upstairs?"

"It doesn't hold much significance to me any longer, Willy. I don't mind what we do with it".

"You wouldn't have said that fifteen years ago, though, would you?"

"No, but in those days, this, and you two, were the only things that I had in the world. This was my world. You could say that this was what defined me… or I defined myself by my family and my possessions. Sad, isn't it. That's something else we can help people realise".

"It's going on the list, my dear. So, the next step is to discuss all this with Becky, I suppose?"

"Yes, after a much needed rest. We've covered a lot of ground, and we've earned a break".

Life in Annwn

13 THE BEGINNING

When Becky arrived, she spent some time looking at the cottage from the outside before going in. Nothing had changed since the last time she had been there, the only difference being that this time she expected to see her parents in their chairs, and that made it easier to see them. She resumed her seat by the fire and greeted them.

"Hello, Mam and Dad. I understand that you have some plans for this old house".

"Yes, we have been given the matter some consideration, but first we would like to know whether you have any thoughts on the matter". They wanted to find out whether she could remember any of the plans they had all discussed before their group was reborn.

"No, I can't even imagine other people, strangers, traipsing around our old home. That's why I've been so loathe to sell it".

Sarah sent a telepathic message to Willy, 'That is how she has rationalised her reluctance anyway, but we know better, don't we? She was aware of our plans subconsciously, but couldn't quite bring it to the fore. That's The Block at work. Sometimes, it works in our favour, sometimes it doesn't. Still, she didn't sell, because she 'knew' that we had other plans for it'.

"It's a very good you didn't sell it, Becky, because with your help and that of others, this little cottage will become a guiding beacon for people in the neighbourhood and even beyond".

"Our little cottage? Really?"

"Yes, there are plans going back long before either you or we were born, plans that you helped lay way back then, but even further back before that, because it was build on Ley Lines and your great grandfather bought it when it was already fairly old. This house and our family have been waiting for us to come along and put it to the purpose for which it was intended. However, over the centuries, minor alterations have been carried out in order to make it more comfortable for the families that were occupying it at at the time, but those changes were inconsequential and can easily be put right.

"The only major change is the construction of a back addition, which can be used for larger assemblies, since the local community is now larger than was originally foreseen. This will take the bulk of the money that we will have to raise. However, once again, first things first. We were thinking of a community drop-in centre for this room during the day, and for special meetings at other times, but basically, it will be a common room.

"The kitchen will remain where it is, but will have to be refurbished to suit the new conditions, which will mean that its primary function will be the provision of tea, coffee, cakes and sandwiches, although there is no need for the cake to be cooked here.

"Then, upstairs, we have the three bedrooms - ours and two small rooms. The small ones would be ideal for more intimate massage sessions, or in circumstances where intense meditation is required. We will occupy our old bedroom, but will allow its use under certain circumstances like Circle Meetings.

"P public prayer meetings and the like will be held either in the garden, weather permitting, or in the proposed new addition".

"What do you think, Becky?" asked her father. "Did you get all that?"

"Yes, I did, Da. I even had a strange sense of Deja Vu, as if we've talked about this before. We have have, haven't we?"

"Yes, a long time ago. You are doing well", said her mother. "Neither your father nor I knew anything about it until we had passed over, so you have a head start... and that is how it should be because you will be the front person here. Everything will need to be signed and approved by you".

"Yes, but don't be alarmed, cariad. We will be with you every step of the way, and there are more behind us too. This is a major development for Spirit in the area in modern times. In fact, we were only discussing the matter with a woman called Julia, er, yesterday? Was that yesterday or today, my dear? And, er, anyway, plans have been laid, and you were involved in that from the start, and now you will be playing the key role in implementing them…"

"Yes… I take it that you are still committed, Becky…"

"Yes, of course. This is really exciting!"

"Good girl, I knew you would be. So, now, your first priority is to recruit help and funding. Have you any thoughts on that?"

"There were some people who went on the prison visits… and there are others who often talk about Dad and the old days, but I wouldn't know how to approach them about this kind of thing… No, that's about it, sorry".

"Don't be sorry, we have kind of sprung this upon you, but you could print off a few flyers and hang them around town for now. Remember, you helped your Dad do the same thing with the visits? Just tell them about your intentions with this place, and ask them to go to a meeting. Hold that in town… in the pub, like you father did.

"There is one other thing that you need to think about quite soon. The contents of this house - what do you want to keep and what will you let go?"

"Let go' as in sell or get rid of?"

"Yes, my dear. It is time to have a clear-out. First off, we don't need anything. However, you might like to keep a few things here for ambiance and use. Like the Welsh dresser and the bay-window table and chairs. Anyway, have a think about it, but everything will have to go to give the builders easy access. Needless to say, if you want to take anything back to your house, it is yours after all".

"Yes, thank you. It just looks right there, I can't imagine it anywhere else".

"You could order a house-clearance, but just make sure that you're there so that they don't take away anything that you want to keep".

"Yes, OK, Dad. I'll work something out".

"OK, darling, well, we'll love you and leave you. The beginning of any major project is difficult, but it will become easier. Have no fear about that. Bye for now!"

'Our old bedroom', she transmitted to Willy, and they both disappeared upstairs.

"Bye, Mam, bye Dad. You can rely on me". She sat looking around herself for five minutes and then left, locking the front door behind her.

∞

A week later, Becky had the whole contents of the house taken away to storage. She didn't feel up to deciding what to keep and what not at that moment, so she put it off. She also printed off the flyers and arranged a meeting for the following Wednesday afternoon after the market, when the pub was at its busiest. Thirty-two people attended that meeting which was twice the number she had expected. She hosted it herself.

"As you know, my father, your friend, William, or Willy, as you better know him, probably, became more open about his Spiritual beliefs in his later years. I know that we all put it down to that Near-death Experience that he had, but the truth of the matter is that he was a deep man and a deep thinker. I don't suppose there's much else for a shepherd to do in this country since they killed off all the wolves - except at lambing.

"Anyway, Dad, and Mam, to be fair to her, had always been quite religious in their own way, but I think, looking back on it, they were too shy to say what they really felt in public… except for Da towards the end, of course.

"So, Dad and I became Spiritualists before he passed away, and I would like to honour his and my mother's memory by turning our old cottage into a Spiritualist Sanctuary. I propose that it be called 'The Spirit of Co-operation', which was something he said to me once.

Becky was skating close to the border of the truth, and she knew it, but she knew no other way of expressing those feelings. At least, she wasn't lying, the consoled herself. Several times, she had to look to her parents standing at the back of the room for moral support, and each time it was given enthusiastically.

"So, I, or we, I should say, are looking for support. Financial is great, but it doesn't have to be that way. We will need to clean and redecorate the place from top to bottom when the alterations are finished - minor though they be. We will also need an addition built on the back or the side of the cottage, so any help there will also be much appreciated.

"Now, I am certain that most of you are wondering what use we are going to put the cottage to, aren't you? Well, we would like it to be a learning centre - somewhere that people can come to learn about life after death and how we think that the world is really set up. Traditional church attendance has been on the wane for decades, and I think that we all know why, so we want to provide an alternative, and we are looking for sponsors, volunteers and well-wishers to help us get the project off the ground!

"What do you say? It can become a meeting place, a drop-in centre, a healing facility, a meditation centre, or just a place to be... you know, where you can just go and sit and no-one will hassle you?

"Somewhere, where you can have a cup of tea and think, or talk to like-minded people. We could have barbecues there in the good weather, and watch the stars for alien spacecraft... We could make things... craft objects that are hard to find these days... we could pass on those skills, and sell the items on line... we could keep the profit, or we could use it to help other people... here or AND abroad... What do you think?

"You have all known me since I was a kid, or I have known you that long. I'm not a hot-head or a scam merchant. This could really work, and all it would take is the thirty-odd of us here... but I know that the movement would grow beyond us thirty. This is our chance to be at the forefront of something big, and I mean that.

"Does anyone have any questions?"

There followed a lively debate in which some people pressed Becky about who the 'we' were that she kept referring to. After a few tense moments, and encouragement from her parents, she admitted that the 'we' increased her parents. There were gasps around the bar, but only from a few. When the people at the meeting dissolved into the public bar, Becky and her parents were completely convinced that they had at least the core of their steering and church committees.

∞

"You handled that extremely well, said her father, when Becky gad resumed her stool by the fire. It was the only stick of furniture left in the building, but being a three-legged affair, it would fit under the stairs easily. Sarah and Willy sat cross-legged on the floor in front of the fire, Kiddy flat out between them.

"Yes, sirree! If I wasn't already in, I'd have joined up on the spot! You handled that to perfection, cariad!" said Willy.

"Indeed, very well done, my dear. I think that you have as good as got your helpers in the bag! You will have to move swiftly now, before they go off the boil. Go around to see them all tomorrow, or as soon as you can, and get them to commit to something... be it money or physical assistance. Write their names on paper in front of them, so that they know.

"Ask them if they want to be founder members, and tell them how much it will cost. I'm afraid that you will have to work that out.

"Then you will need another meeting in order to set a plan for the restoration process and how to raise the money to pay for it, but don't worry too much about that yet. Issue Press Releases to the local and county newspapers too, and ask interested parties to contact you.

"Let's see what that brings in. You could also write to local and county businesses asking for their support, and talk to the local paper about regular, say weekly, progress reports..."

"Yes, Becky, keep the project bubbling under people's noses", added her father.

∞

While Becky was busy writing text for the newspaper articles and the flyers, her parents were hard at work keeping Julia and their friends informed of their progress, and scouting the Brecon Beacons for signs that hitherto uninterested people had become interested in Spiritualism. It was a growing trend in many walks of life and always had been popular in Wales, which was well-known for its ancient Druids and its Celtic mysticism. Many of the local population only paid lip service to the established churches, going their own way as their ancestors had before them. Annwn was not a widely known concept in the area, but only because a lot of people didn't know the name Annwn and where it originated from. It was fair to say that the average church-goer in Brecon was not the same as his or her counterpart in London.

Under those circumstances, it was not difficult to raise enough money to have the cottage converted to its new use, and even go out to seek tenders for the extension. Becky, for her husband, John, was not interested in the property if he could not sell it, sought tenders from five local builders, all of whom were recommended by the Steering Committee.

All of the tenders were competitive, but one was outstanding. A firm called Marlyn Construction Services, from out of town, offered to build the extension completely free of charge and supply the materials at cost price. Upon closer negotiations, it transpired that the boss of the company and his four sons were Spiritualists and would carry out the necessary renovation themselves in their free time, which meant that it would take longer to complete. After a short committee meeting, their offer was gratefully accepted and the documents were signed.

The Spirit of Co-operation was on its way!

∞

"What do you think, Sarah? It's going to be strange to share our home with a load of strangers, isn't it?"

"Yes", she chuckled, "I never really liked having visitors when I lived here before. But now it's going to be an open house!"

"I suppose that we still have our little bedroom sanctuary… well, for most of the time".

"Yes, but none of it is a problem really. We can just spin off into another parallel universe, can't we. I mean, there's nothing to say that we have to remain in this one, just because it will be where we will be doing most of our work. We can commute in from… er, elsewhere, anywhere, any time!" and the both laughed out loud.

If there had been sheep in the field, they might have turned their heads to see what the all the fuss was about…

14 THE DREAM TAKES FORM

Once all the furniture and possessions had been taken to storage, the cottage looked as no-one had seen it since it was first built more than two hundred years before, when William's forebears had moved in. Even without any contents, the cottage still had a pleasing, lived-in, cosy atmosphere about it. When she had been boxing up the contents, Becky had found old toys that made her cry, an empty packet of cigarettes, the brand of which she didn't recognise, and rightly assumed that it must have been her grandfather's. She ran her hands through a rack of her mother's old dresses, very few by modern standards, knowing that her father had not been able to bring himself to take them to the charity shop, and she found old shoes that she was sure she had never seen before.

It was a very slow process, which took her days longer than she had allocated. Friends had offered to help, but she didn't want to be hurried or made to feel foolish. She was enjoying her trip down Memory Lane. It would be the last time, so she knew that she had to make the most of it.

On the first Saturday afternoon after the clearance, Becky led the Steering Committee around the empty house and told them what she and her parents had thought was probably the best use for each room, and later, seated on some stackable garden furniture she had brought along, they went through suggestions.

Mr. Davies thought that new plastic windows and exterior doors should be a priority to discourage squatters, a problem that he saw could only get worse with people losing their homes in the cities. People agreed, so Becky wrote it in her desk diary as something to be discussed with

Life in Annwn

Marlyn.

Mrs. James, who owned a tearoom in the village, suggested slabbing an area in the back garden, so that people could sit outside to take refreshments in good weather, and a teenage boy named Alec asked that there be an area at the far end of the garden where they could celebrate Bonfire Night. However, Mr. Brown, a hill farmer, said that fireworks were a waste of money and only served to frighten the sheep grazing nearby. A lively discussion ensured, until Becky suggested that they should only be talking about essential matters at the moment.

When the meeting had closed and every had gone, Becky phoned Marlyn and arranged a consultation for the coming Monday.

Sarah and Willy appeared before her. "Hello both, I didn't notice you before, have you been here long?"

"No, we've just arrived", said Willy, "how did the meeting go?"

"Very well, I think. Nobody warned to change anything that we had suggested, and there were a few sensible suggestions too. I've put them on a list to discuss with Marlyn on Monday. Er, I had to take the committee into your room, I hope you don't mind".

"No, not at all… there's going to be worse done to it than that over the coming weeks, so don't fret about it", said Sarah. It's strange to see our old home like this, isn't it? Sort of naked…" It was so unusual to hear Sarah talk like that, that Becky felt a little shocked. "It will soon take on the role for which it was ultimately intended - a symbol of hope, help, co-operation and Spiritual growth for the people who live nearby. It already has a power all of its own. It sits on Ley Lines like the pyramids of the Ancient World, and it will harness or rather channel those natural forces or the Earth, just as the pyramids were intended to. This is our prism of metaphorical Light. Now all we need to do is get the right people to run it from the physical Plane, because the helpers on the Spiritual Plane have been waiting to take up their roles for a long while already - in Earth time".

Neither Willy nor Becky had ever seen Sarah look so magical and profound. At least, Willy already knew part of the plans, but Sarah had

Becky completely Mesmerised. She looked to her father for guidance, but he was practically in the same boat.

Sarah had seemed to come out of her trance-like state when she said to Becky, "Have you thought about what colours you will paint the place?"

"Er, no, Mam, do you have any suggestions?"

"Yes, I think that I do… we want warm colours. Emulsion, and gloss paint, perhaps satin finish not high gloss. Wood stain and preservative for the rafters, of course, where they are visible, and perhaps… not white or magnolia… er, orange is too much… an off-white with orange, perhaps peach… something like that. If they don't sell it, we can have it made up for us… and a light yellow for the door frames and doors. The plastic windows and exterior doors… I appreciate the idea of security - that is a good point, but we don't really want any inorganic materials in the house".

"Hardwood?" suggested Willy.

"Yes, hardwood would be ideal… stained to match the rafters… and a light-oak floor-covering… and kitchen cabinets. That will match the pine dresser and other bits of furniture that we will bring back. How is the roof?"

"I don't know, Mam".

"It wasn't leaking before…" added Willy, "that's best quality Welsh slate that is. It'll last another thirty or forty years… we only had it recovered twenty-five years ago! I think".

"Yes, if it needs to be repaired, they have to use Welsh slate to match, Becky. Make certain that they understand that".

Becky was not taking notes, but she was trying to remember what her mother was saying. She was also thinking about the cost. Her mother hadn't mentioned anything that was cheap yet. "That is going to be quite a shopping list, Mam! Custom hardwood doors and windows, custom paint and emulsion..Welsh slate…"

"Yes, I know, but the correct ambiance is extremely important! It would be senseless to spoil hundreds of years of planning for the sake of a few extra shillings, wouldn't it? Anyway, you and your volunteers can apply the paint and emulsion, so you will make a significant saving there".

When Becky looked to her father for support, he only shrugged and pressed his lips tight together as if to say, ' You know what she's like'.

"Yes, I understand your misgivings, but just have faith. When we know what we need, we can start to plan how to raise the money we will need, but you can rest assured that Spirit did not plan all this, for all this time, and involve so many people, just to be beaten at the final fence by a little bit of money!

"Oh, no! That will not happen… definitely not! Your next job, Becky is to have all this work costed, so that you know how much you need to raise. However, you do know that you will have to raise something, so you could get on with that and recruit others to help you".

Becky knew that her most difficult task was about to begin and didn't really relish having to ask people for donations. Her mother read her mind.

"Don't worry, my dear, most people in the vicinity will realise that the Sanctuary is actually for their benefit, and the costs might not be as high as you imagine".

Sarah and Willy disappeared leaving Becky with her thoughts.

∞

When Becky went to meet the builders on Monday morning, she took an old camping table with and arrived an hour early. She had bought an A4 hardback notebook for the project, and set about drawing lines to define the page margins while she gathered her thought. Then she entered the date, the location and the purpose of the entry, and listed the points that her mother had made the last time she had been there.

When Mr Jones of Marlyn Construction Services Limited arrived, he had two of his sons with him and his own notebook.

"Good afternoon, Mrs. Day, I'd like to introduce Rhys and Huw. They are going to help me measure up. If you'll show me the size and position of the addition, they can go and take some measurements".

Becky experienced a mild panic, as that hadn't been discussed with her parents, but she went outside with the men and thought about her mother.

"Where do you want to locate it, Mrs. Day?"

"Oh, please call me Becky, everyone does," she said looking up from her non-existent notes. To her massive delight, her parents were standing behind the cottage defining two corners using their arms in L-shapes. When she didn't reply immediately, Mr. Jones tried to be helpful.

"Where does the worst weather come from? You could use the back addition to shield the garden from that". Becky watched her mother and father nodding, still holding their arms up. Becky led the builders to the proposed corners and Rhys stuck pegs in the ground where she indicated.

"OK, Becky, we can leave them to get on with that, and you can show me around inside. I'm Colin by the way".

When Becky had given him the grand tour and spoken of the colour scheme, she went into the kitchen to brew four mugs of tea. Colin called his sons in to join them when it had been poured.

They discussed the proposed work, and Becky reiterated her stipulations for the materials.

"What about the extension, Becky? Stone to match the cottage would be terribly expensive, although it could be done".

"I hadn't thought about that, could you price for stone, block and brick, or is ghat being cheeky?"

"No, that isn't a problem… and the roof?"

"Oh, yes, well I do know that my, er, partners want Welsh slate to match our roof".

"OK, a traditional roof or trellises?"

Becky was lost now, but said that she would let them know later that day.

"With a ceiling, I take it. How high?"

"I will let you know those details within a few hours too, Colin".

Satisfied that they had enough details to be going on with, especially after Becky had rung later, the Jones' left and Becky sat at the table to write up her notes.

As she had expected, her parents soon joined her.

"That all went very well, cariad, well done!" said her father

"Yes, I agree, well done, darling. So, that is all in hand. The only thing that bothers me still is matching the new building with the old one. The stone, limestone, they used for this house is common enough in these parts. I'm sure that we could lay our hands on some easily enough…"

"Even if we only had enough for the outside skin, the inside one could be of cheap concrete blocks…"

"I've got it! There's that old dilapidated dry stone wall that used to separate two of our fields a little way up the mountain. Don't you remember? When it started to fall down, we didn't bother to repair it because it gave the sheep easier access to more grazing land. I bet there's enough up there, and if we're a bit short, well, I'm sure that Mr Jones can pick some more up from the quarry. If a gang of volunteers went up there with a small tipper, it would probably only take two journeys, I bet it would be cheaper than buying new blocks too!"

"You never cease to surprise me, Sarah, I must say. You always seem to have all the answers".

"That's what you think because I speak the words, but that doesn't mean that the solutions are mine. There are more than just we three working on this project, as I have said before. To you are Becky, I appear to be the genius, but to the friends of the Spirit of Co-operation, it will to be Becky. People localise things, it makes them easier to conceptualise, but there is usually more going on than the average person realises".

Becky and Willy looked at each other as Sarah walked off to inspect a wall, and felt as if they had been told. They both understood at that moment that there was more to Sarah than they had ever given her credit for when they knew her on Earth.

"Just as I thought", she said surprising them again, and tapping the wall with her knuckles, "this plaster has blown… it's come away from the stonework. Let's hope that there are only isolated patches".

∞

Five days later, an envelope arrived from Marlyn containing a sketch of the proposed extension with some important dimensions and a tender with several options for the extension walls.

"On top of this price, you will want decorative materials, which we offered to supply at trade price. For the time being, we suggest purchasing one hundred litres - five tubs - ten litres of white undercoat, five litres of gloss/satin, and five litres of wood-stain preservative.

"Please phone me at your earliest convenience to arrange a convenient time for us to meet so that we can go through the tender".

Becky was not sure whether the price was high, too high or reasonable, but she wanted to take it to her Steering Committee first anyway, so she rang the members of that first to arrange a meeting.

"Keep it up, girl, your mother and I are right behind you. She's telling me to tell you not to worry about the money. Oh, well. Easy for her to say, I suppose, but I have every faith in her. She never let you down. Remember that, and neither will I", see you soon.

Life in Annwn

15 LOST TREASURE

"What?! £25,000 to turn your old cottage into a place fit to worship...? I think that that sounds quite expensive", opined Bob Brown, a farmer. "I think my boys could do it cheaper than that".

"You have the right to tender for the work, Mr Brown", said Becky, "but that price includes the extension too, all the materials and labour. Not only that, but the materials are all top notch... no cheap stuff".

"My boys wouldn't use cheap stuff either! If you wanted to pay the extra. You only get what you pay for!"

"Exactly, Mr Brown. Are going to submit a tender?"

"That's not very fair, is it?" said Mrs. Davies. Marlyns did the drawing free and at their own expense and you get to use it free..."

"And, you've had a gander at their prices. No, that's not fair tendering practice at all. Anyway, Mr Jones is a professional..."

"My boys is professional too".

"Yes, professional pigmen! Not builders, not your actual professional builders, are they?"

"They've done all the work on Fferm Cartref, and there's nothing wrong with it! Nothing at all. You can come and inspect it if you like!"

"Oh, don't get so aeriated, Bob, you'll do yourself a mischief. No-one's calling your boys cowboys, I'm sure they are quite capable of building a cowshed or a pig-pen, but we want something prestigious. People might come from miles around... Have your boys got the time to put into a project like that? Winter'll be on us as soon as we know it, Bob..."

"Yes, and we don't want no hold-ups... not with our weather up here, and your even more exposed up there, ain't you, Becky?"

"We get it all up at the cottage, yes".

Life in Annwn

"You don't want the roof half on and half off when it starts to blow a hooley! It could cost a lot of money in damages. Do you have that sort of insurance, Bob?"

"Well, maybe my boys is a bit busy to be taking on any new projects at this time of the year... but it would have been nice to be asked! That's the point I'm making. We got to pay fir it, so we should have a say where the money goes. That's only right and proper".

"Yes, all right, Mr Brown, your point has been duly noted. Are there any other comments? In that case, I move for a vote to accept Marlyn's tender. Can I see a show of hands. Thank you, carried unanimously. Thank you ladies and gentlemen.

"I'll get this letter off to Mr Jones tomorrow morning, and I suggest that we call this meeting to a close, and go for a drink. I believe Frank wants to open this bar at eight, and it's ten to now".

Everyone adjourned to the public bar of the Red Dragon pub in the village, and the landlady, Sue, nipped in to give the room a final clean before her customers started to arrive. It was the quiz night and that usually filled the room - it was one of the highlights of the local social calendar.

∞

Becky got the acceptance letter off to Marlyn the following morning and then started calling around the members of the Steering Committee to see who had decided to become Founding Members of The Spirit of Co-operation. The committee had discussed the matter at the meeting, and decided to give themselves the first chance, since they were doing all the work. The fee had been set at £1,000 per head, but people could donate more if they had a mind to. They were looking for a maximum of twenty-five founding members, which would mean that they would have very fundraising to do if they were successful. There were only eleven on the committee, which gave plenty of scope for other locals to apply, but £11,000 would give them an immediate lump sum with which to commence the refurbishment.

By lunchtime, she had five definites, including herself, although her husband didn't know about it at that precise moment, and three probablies. One had pleaded poverty, and two had been unreachable hitherto. After a spot of lunch, she began work on a recruitment poster to find the remaining fifteen members.

∞

On the following Saturday morning, Mr Jones arrived driving a three-ton flatbed lorry with a Kabota digger on it. "Rhys will pull those footings out in no time!" he said laughing, "This thing is his baby, and nobody can handle it better. You watch him lull the muck out with the back actor. Have you got anywhere up here we can dispose of the spoil, Becky. It would save a lot of time if we don't have to take it away?"

"I don't know, I, er, hadn't thought about…" then her mother's voice came into her head, "Use it to line the wall behind the extension and across the back garden fence. You can turn it into raised flower beds".

Becky explained the idea. "That would provide a beautiful show of flowers".

"Good idea! Tipping us so frightfully expensive these days, especially if we'd had to take the muck off the mountain". Colin had a word with Rhys and the banks man they had brought up on overtime for the day, and then went inside with Huw and his labourer. "Huw is our plasterer-cum-jack-of-all-trades, but this morning, he's going to be marking off patches of blown plaster for renewal. There'll be a bit of dust involved, Becky, so if you want to leave us to it, that's fine by me".

"OK, what time will you be finishing?"

"Oh, it's nine o'clock now, so about one, I think. The labourers like their Saturday afternoons in the pub - it's a bit of a traditional, see".

"Yes, well, if you want to come down to the village pub when you're done, I'll start their afternoon off for them myself".

"We'll see how it goes, but that is very kind of you, Becky. We'll see you later, even if it's only to drop the keys off".

"Oh, that isn't necessary, you can hang onto those, but I won't hold you up any longer. Perhaps, I'll see you all later".

∞

Becky went about her normal Saturday morning business looking after her family and getting the shopping in fir the weekend, but remembered to go to the Dragon at one to see if the builders were in. They weren't, but she decided to give them until two, before carrying on with her matriarchal chores. The five men arrived at one thirty. Two were covered in a pinkish dust, which she guessed was the plaster, since one of the men was Huw, and the other three were splashed with mud, although they had cleaned their boots. They attracted quite a lot of attention, since most of the drinkers knew that work on the cottage had been due to start that day.

"What are you having?" she asked the happy, smiling bunch of workers.

"There's no need, Becky. Thanks anyway. I'll get these", said Colin.

"No, you won't! You've been working up there all morning for nothing - for nothing!" she repeated raising her voice, "and you've driven up from Barry. We wouldn't hear of it, would we?"

A few people around them shook their heads, but it was Becky who took the money out to pay. "In that case, five pints of bitter, please.

"Go and have a look around", he told his four mates, when they had sipped their drinks and said 'Cheers!'. "I want a chat with Becky, a minute.

"We pulled out the footings easily enough, and chopped out most, if not all of the loose plaster. We don't have any more time, and no materials anyway to carry on this weekend, but we will send gear up during the week, and we will do next Saturday and Sunday mornings. Anyway, that's the progress report, now the interesting bit. We found all this in the spoil coming out of the foundations". Colin handed Becky a crisp packet that was too heavy to contain potato chips. "I suggest that you go up there and look in the walls of the founds we've dug out, and in the spoil heap. There could be more.

"Don't walk-on the edge of the footings though, eh. We don't want them collapsing and someone getting hurt. We've put some blocks down for you to gain access - a little stairway.

"Come on, lads, we'd best be off. I'm getting to like it here too much. If you are looking for something to do during the week, you could clean up inside, and pick the rocks out of the spoil heap - they may come in handy for the stone wall.

"See you next week".

"Yes, thank you, Colin, and you, lads". As she watched them leave, she realised that she had much more to say and ask. She was feeling quite stunned and then she remembered the bag in her hand.

He doesn't mess about, does he?" said Frank looking at the door they had just disappeared through. That pint hardly touched the sides. What's in the bag, Becks? Not half a bag of crisps, surely?"

Becky tipped the contents out onto the bar. Frank gasped and Becky's eyes opened wide. "Well, would you believe it!" he said slowly in utter amazement.

Becky picked up the brooch he was probably referring to. It was a silver cat in three-quarter profile with two red stones for eyes. Its tail was held straight up in the air, but there was a kink in the end of it. She turned it over and over in her fingers, and then gave it to the landlord, while she examined silver and copper coins, and what looked like a gold toothpick.

"And these all came out of a trench in your back garden?" said one of the locals who had been following developments.

"It seems so, Tom, yes. I love that cat, let's have another look".

"At least he's honest. A lot of people would have kept them and not told you!"

"Yes, that's true…" said Becky, nodding. "He seems a very nice man… and his sons and staff. Yes, I was impressed with them all, but I didn't expect this…"

"Why's that?" asked Sue. "Does the brooch mean anything to you?"

"Er, no, no. I've never heard anything about it before. Intriguing, though, isn't it? The cat's eyes grab your attention. They force you to look back at it"."

"Ooh, yes! So they do! It's a bit spooky, if you ask me."

"Yes, Johnny, what can I get you, love? Same again, is it?"

"Pay no attention to her", said Frank sotto voce, "our Sue's superstitious about cats. I think it's very nice, for what that's worth. Same again, Becky, is it? You look as if you could do with it".

"Er, yes, please, Frank, but make it a double this time, and then I have to go see to the kids".

∞

When she arrived home, her sons were watching sport on TV in the lounge. She had left their lunch before she had gone out in the morning, and there were snacks in the fridge. They didn't need her for anything, and were even slightly surprised to see her, but she had known all that anyway. She wanted to know more about the beguiling cat, so she was hoping to talk to her parents. She called them to her bedroom, since John was in Cardiff, and they came.

"Marlyn Construction has been working this morning and look what they found in the ground! Isn't it gorgeous?"

"It's a She, darling, not an it", said her mother sitting down to look at it lying on the table.

"Have you seen it before, Mam?"

"No, not I, well, not before this morning. We saw Colin find it we were watching the dig. I think he saw us too, but we didn't speak".

"Do you know anything about it, Da?"

"When I was a boy, my grandmother used to tell of a cat with firestone eyes, but they were just stories to me".

"The cat with firestone eyes", repeated Becky."That sounds really spooky".

"Do you remember any of those stories? I'd love to hear them".

"No, alas, I haven't thought about them for nigh on seventy years…"

"Oh, don't be mean, Willy! Tell the poor girl!"

"Well, it is true, that I had forgotten about the cat, but we've been researching the brooch since we saw Colin find it, and we do have some information. Apparently, it belonged to my great grandmother, so your great, great grandmother and she insisted that it be buried in the garden. We think that people said OK to humour her, but then one night when everyone was asleep, she did bury it and wouldn't tell anyone where, and since they didn't miss the brooch for weeks, there was little chance of finding it. Soon afterwards, people gave up and forgot. However, Great Grandmother Megan was putting her cat with the firestorm eyes safe for one who would come later.

"Unfortunately, she was a bit doolally twp by then, so nobody took any notice of what she said".

"Great, great granny Megan, eh, put this cat away for me to find… how long ago, do you think?"

"They say that a generation is twenty-five years, so about a hundred and fifty years ago perhaps. All that part of the family has been reborn, so we can't talk to anyone, well, it's not nice to disturb them, but we will keep looking. Interesting, isn't it?"

"I love her", said Becky and her mother agreed.

"Before the NHS came about, doctors were expensive and tended to stay near rich people in the cities, poor folk relied on Wise Women, and men, who knew herbs and local plants. They made potions and medicines, and charged very little. Life was like that for thousands of years, until a lot of the old ladies, and their not so old apprentices, began to be persecuted by the established churches as witches. Many of they gave up their practices, others went underground. The last prosecution for sorcery was in 1944 and one of the things they were said to be known by was their cat, which was a familiar".

"Are you saying that Great, great, granny Megan was a witch?"

Life in Annwn

"She could well have been a White Witch… possibly even a Black one, judging by some of your father's relatives…"

"Eh, I heard that!"

"You were meant to…"

16 A DRAWING BECOMES REALITY

Becky and a varying team of committee members and her sons spent the week sifting through the mound of excavated earth looking for more artefacts, an putting the rocks aside for dressing for the wall, while Bob's boys and a few others transported three wagon loads of old dry stone walling down to the cottage. By the following Saturday morning, the back garden was looking quite organised, if not tidy. The builders merchant had also delivered three palettes of nine-inch concrete blocks, one of engineering bricks, twenty bags of cement and a ton of sand.

It was a scene set or action, and when Marlyn's men arrived in the morning, they got straight to work. They did two half days, and when they left, the oversite - the foundations and the concrete slab - was complete and the patches in the plaster had been put right. The interior of the old cottage was ready for redecoration.

Becky and the committee were very impressed; even Bob had to admit that, so they organised a painting gang, which started work on the Monday morning at ten o'clock. They had great fun working two or three to a room, so as not to get under each other's feet, but a portable radio could be heard all over the house blaring out popular music from the Seventies and Eighties. Most people joined in with their favourites, which created a fantastic atmosphere - something that the Thais call 'sanuk' or 'joy at work', a word unavailable in the English language.

In three days they had applied two coats of emulsion to the walls, stained the rafters and undercoated the woodwork. Then on Thursday, they glossed the doors, frames and skirting, leaving Friday to clean the house up.

The windows and exterior doors were still being made and wouldn't be fitted for a fortnight, but they could easily cut in around those when the time came.

Becky sold the Founding Memberships fairly quickly, and easily, although not all of the Founding Members took as active a role as she would have liked, but then some of them were quite old, and could not be expected to climb ladders!

Two gangs of bricklayers worked from diagonally opposite corners of the extension, and they managed to complete six courses of blocks a morning, meaning that the inner skin went up in a weekend. The external skin of stonework took longer, but Huw and his men could work on the inside. They soon had the walls plastered and the floor screeded, while Gareth and his team fitted the trusses and slated it over. In six weeks of mostly weekend work, they had the cottage and extension complete, and ready for Becky and her happy band to decorate.

They opened the cottage and extension to the public with a small ceremony, and then all retired to the village pub, much to the delight of the landlord and his wife, although they had been very supportive throughout, and always provided as much assistance as they could.

"I take it that you were brought up in that cottage, Becky", said Colin over a drink in the Red Dragon.

"Yes, my parents left it to me, or at least my Dad did when he passed away four months ago. My Mam died quite a while back now. What makes you ask?"

"Oh, it's easy really. In fact, I have been meaning to mention it for months, but never got around to it. When we were working up there that first day, and I found those bits and pieces, I notice that you wear the cat brooch often now… it suits you… could have been made for you… Anyway, that first day… I saw two elderly people watching us working. I suppose they were about thirty feet away. They were standing close together, so I assumed that they were man and wife, in their sixties, I imagine, and dressed in the old style. They didn't say anything, just watched, but I got the impression that they were content. Does that ring any bells?"

"Thank you. I love this brooch, and it's funny, but I do feel as if I was meant to have it. I only wish that I knew more about it. The couple you saw could have been my parents, I always see my Dad as he was when he died in his early Seventies, but I see my mother a lot younger, about sixty years old…"

"Is that them over there watching us now?"

Becky looked up and followed his line of sight. "Yes. I see them often. The 'Spirit of Co-operation' was their idea. They say that it will become a beacon for humanity".

"A beacon in the Beacons! I like it!"

"I hadn't thought of that… a Beacon of Light for humanity in the Brecon Beacons! It sounds awfully grand when you put it like. So, you can see Spirit too".

"Yes, I always have been able to; and my sisters and my parents can. Well, my Dad's been dead for sixty years, and my mother for forty. My Dad was scared of what he saw, it was an unwelcome gift for him, poor man. He used to go to the pub to distract himself from the visions, but my mother took to it like you have".

"I was a late-comer, but I embrace it gladly now. While I'm thinking about it, how much do we owe you, Colin? You and your men have done a wonderful job. We're ever so grateful".

"Don't worry about the money for now. I'll send you the final bill next week".

"Will you come to some of our meetings?"

"Yes, it would be an honour. If you let me know when, I'll do my best to get here. Now, I'd better round up the lads and get them back to Barry, before it gets late, or I'm tempted to have another pint", and so saying, he took his leave of Becky and their new friends and left with the boys waving from the open back of the lorry.

When the committee considered the bill at the end of the week, even Bob had to admit that his boys probably couldn't have done a better job or for a cheaper price.

Life in Annwn

∞

"What do you think of the old place now, Willy?" asked Sarah as they were seated before their fire.

He screwed up his nose. "It's not quite the same, is it? Not quite so homely as we had it before… it's too empty for me".

"Yes, I know what you mean. Still, that's easy to fix. Just imagine it like it was. Is that better?"

"Yes, that's much more like it. I feel home again now… I mean, the new decor is fine… it suits a church, but a church is not a home, is it?"

"They call it The House of God".

"That's true enough, well, He's welcome to it. Perhaps He's Mediterranean - they like bleak, minimalist walls, don't they - but I like a cluttered house that looks as if it has been lived in. This will do me… God can live in the extension!" Sarah reached out and touched his hand.

"I don't know about God being a Mediterranean, but Jesus and his family definitely were, and I doubt whether they had enough stuff to clutter their houses with".

"You're probably right there, love. So, what is next on the agenda?"

"Next? Well, this project is not finished yet, not by a long chalk. I have never seen the end of this one, so I am assuming that it will go on for many decades to come. Who knows, perhaps even for ever?

"The next thing to do here is to get the community charged up… to activate, incentivise them… to build a Community Spirit, as it is so rightly called… and that means organising events… events on all levels, so that everyone, from beginners to the ambitious can find something to motivate them.

"You don't want to bewilder the novice and you don't want to bore the acolyte".

"That sounds a lot like the Seven Planes you often mention".

"Yes, well, the concept is in evidence everywhere you look, but people don't look. Most people are unobservant… just like I was when I lived here on The Surface. Still, living and learning, that's what it's all about… everything else is a waste of time".

"Isn't that a bit harsh, cariad? People need to relax and let their hair down sometimes…"

"I suppose so, but there is nothing wrong with a balanced life, but the balance is way off in most people's case. Part of our task, yours, mine and Becky's, is to try to reset that balance".

"What sort of a role do you foresee for me? I mean, I can see you as team leader, and I can see Becky as Spirit's Earthly representative, but where do I fit into this vast Eternal Plan?"

"I appreciate your confidence in me, darling, but I do not know everything. My advice is to trust in Spirit. This part of The Plan was a very long time ago - they won't have left you out! I'm pretty sure about that! Just work on your own development and be ready to help others, and you will find your way".

"If you say so, my dear".

"You seem a bit down, Willy…"

"No, not really… well, maybe, a little… When I was out on the mountain with the sheep, there was nothing I enjoyed more than getting home in the evening, having something to eat, and then putting my feet up in front of the fire, but it's not the same now, because I don't do anything! Don't get me wrong, cariad, I love sitting talking with you. I have missed this for so long, but I need to do more… I was an active man… before".

"All right, do you want to go out?"

"Go where? The pub? Or somewhere like that?"

"No, not quite, but socialising, yes".

"Yes, all right! Where are we going?"

"Into town. Take my hand, and let's go".

Willy found himself outside the Tower of Learning moments later, still holding his wife's hand. Some people arrived yesterday and I think you'd get a kick out of meeting them". She hesitated a moment and then said, "Room 401" and they left again. "Ready? Let's go in". Willy pushed open the heavy door, and could hear a low buzz of voices. There were about fifty people in the room talking in small groups as at a reception.

"Who are they?" asked Willy, "Do you know any of them?"

"No, not actually know, but I have met a few of them before. A new term is starting soon, and most of these are visiting students and teachers".

"Are you in this class?"

"No, there students are a few levels above me, but we all get together sometimes. This is like the first evening back after the summer holidays, if it helps to think of it in Surface terms".

"Yes, but if they are a few years in advance of you, then they are going to be way ahead of me, aren't they?"

"Er, well, yes and no. It isn't very helpful to think of it like that. The analogy with a Surface university is rather tenuous, but it's the only one I can think of at the moment.

"Ah, Sowell, how are you?" she said to an androgynous young person who was passing close by. He looked human, but his colouring was slightly unusual and his facial features were different. He was not unhandsome, but he would have drawn many stares walking down the streets of Cardiff. Willy heard a voice in his head, "Hello, Sarah, nice to see you again. You look positively radiant, as ever".

"Thank you, Sowell", she replied moving her lips."You are looking well too. All ready to begin the next phase, are you? This is Willy, we were married on The Surface the last time around".

"Hello, Willy! Any friend of Sarah's is a friend of mine". This time he moved his lips in case telepathy was not Willy's strongest skill.

"Nice to meet you, Sowell", he replied not moving his. "I can hear you even though not perfectly yet".

"You stick with it. Sarah is a good teacher, and you'll soon make progress. Anyway, please excuse me, I have to talk with someone over there".

"Who was that?" asked Willy.

"Sowell? He's a student here".

"Where's he from? He doesn't look as if he's from around here…"

"Don't be rude!" she said slapping his shoulder playfully.

"I wasn't being, but he's obviously not, is he?"

"No, but he has been studying here for a very long time. I forget where he's actually from, but it is very far away I've never been there".

They spend a little while mingling with the others, but Willy had never been a socialite on The Surface, and that characteristic was still embedded in him. He tried though, but was mostly in awe of the different colours and sizes the attendees came in. They were all vaguely humanoid, but they definitely were not all the same, and they were definitely not from Earth. Some didn't even bother to wear bodies - they were just light, although they had donned features presumably to make it easier for less advanced souls to determine their mood. When Willy asked to be taken home, Sarah had been waiting for it for a while.

"You can stay if you like, Sarah, but you know that this sort of thing is not my cup of tea, or, better still, take me home and then you come back. I can see that you're enjoying yourself".

"Nah, that's all right. We can go home. I, well, we, will see these people around from time to time now that they're back

in Annwn, but I am glad that we have shown our faces.

"Come on, let's slip away".

Back in front of their fire, Willy said, "I don't know, Sarah, but now that we're home again, I realise that I did enjoy meeting your friends, it was just very stressful at the time. It was very strange to be at reception like that and not have a drink or a paper plate of food in my hands. I felt at a loss what to do with my hands. Like an ex-smoker, I suppose… That's what they say, isn't it? That they miss holding something in their hand".

"Yes, they do. Drinkers don't like staying in pubs without a drink either, do they?"

"No, I suppose not… it's not what you're used to, is it? Old habits die hard… same as those old soldiers at the inn".

"Yes, and the big bull elephant and his little stake…"

"That's slightly different, drinks and fags are props…"

"OK, if you like".

"No, chwarae teg, fair play! I can see where you're coming from too. Do you think that I should enrol in school too?"

"It doesn't really matter what I think, darling. You should do what you think is best. You know my motto though, don't you? Onwards and Upwards!"

"Yes, dear. I think that it would be a good idea, but for now, I'm not going to worry about it, I'm going to recharge my batteries. See you later, my dear".

"Rest well, my darling!"

Willy soon drifted off, but Sarah continued to stare into the fire's dancing flames for some time longer planning how to best put their new asset, 'The Spirit of Co-operation', to the best use of the community. She knew that she had support in the village, and in Annwn, but she wanted to enlist more help - possibly from her off-world foreign student friends.

17 THE FIRESTONE-EYED CAT

"Willy, have you thought about being reborn onto The Surface?"

"No, not at all, but I wouldn't know how to go about it anyway... Isn't it a bit soon though? I mean, I haven't been here long have I?"

"No, but depending on what you want to achieve, the organisation can take a very long time... especially if there are any special skills that you need to learn before you go back there. So, it doesn't hurt to start thinking about it early".

"OK, darling, I'll take your word for it. I know that you're right... I know that I can trust you".

"Thanks, are you ready to go to see Becky?"

"Yes, certainly. I suddenly have the feeling that she's going to ask about that brooch, do you?"

"That's wonderful, Willy. Yes, I just felt that too. She is very pleased with it, we'll have to do some research into it for her. You don't know anything about it, do you?"

"No, I feel as if I ought to though. When I look at it pinned to Becky's breast, it almost speaks to me... it almost says 'Hello'... I feel that well acquainted with it".

"Have you noticed that your Block is lifting, Willy?"

"I am aware of something. It is as if a fog is lifting and the world around me is making more sense... I almost want to say that it's like a poor telephone line has been fixed and I am beginning to hear the other party... parties more clearly".

"Yes, that is it!" she exclaimed with obvious joy in her voice. Most people on The Surface live their lives in relative isolation... cut off from their links to every other living thing in Existence, but here, the more evolved you are, the more you are able to expand those connections. You were well-connected before… in our sense of the word before you returned to The Surface, but The Block has taken a long time to lift this time. It is indeed like a fog lifting, like light being allowed back into your life.

"Come on then, let's go to see our daughter".

After their training session, Becky was keen to tell them about the progress at the cottage. It didn't seem to register with her that they were probably keeping abreast of events out of their own interest. However, they didn't interrupt her, because they were interested to learn how she saw the way things were panning out.

"That is excellent news, Becky", said her mother. "So, you foresee a lot of people in the village taking an active part?"

"Oh, yes! I haven't encountered any opposition at all, not that I would have expected any. Dad did such a lot of the groundwork with his prison visits… they changed people's lives both in the village and the prison. We need to restart that programme, because, well, it sort of petered out after you passed on, Dad. We all gave up, unfortunately.

"Have you noticed my brooch?"

"Yes, it's beautiful", replied Sarah. "You showed it to us once before and I have noticed you wearing it. It suits you".

"Oh, yes! That's right… Mr Jones, the builder, gave it to me. He found it in one of the trenches on the first day. Do either of you know anything about it? He told me that he saw you watching them working from time to time".

"I said I thought he could see us, didn't I, Sarah?"

"Yes, The Block is definitely lifting. Why don't you tell Becky what you know about the brooch?" Willy did so.

"You, know, I'd like to know more about it too, Sarah. It's fascinating, isn't it?"

"Yes. I've never seen one like it before. OK, we'll see what we can do. When we have left, put the brooch in a small empty jewellery box, or a plastic bag, and leave it on your dresser. It is best that it is not in contact with other items when we have it inspected. I don't know when that will take place, so, please leave it in its container until I tell you."

"But how long will that take, Mam? I have become so attached to it that I hate to take it off even when I go to bed. I feel as if I have been wearing it all my life".

"I don't know, my dear, a day or two or three…"

Becky pouted, sighed and turned the brooch to look at her. Its eyes seemed to twinkle at her. "OK".

"Good, well, we ought to be going now, but we'll be back to see you soon. Goodbye, darling".

"Bye, both", she said still looking the cat in the eyes. "I'm going to miss you!" she said softly and kissed it on the nose.

"Bye, cariad!" she heard the disembodied voice of her father say, "I'm as interested in finding out as you are".

∞

"Where are we going now, boss?" asked Willy as they were on the wing. "Back to our place?"

"Please don't call me that, even in jest, dear. I don't like it. No, I thought that we might as well strike while the iron is hot. Let's go to Annwn and look for some help with that brooch We could try my old teacher.

"Room 201", she said after stopping outside the Tower of Learning for a brief moment. She pushed the door to the classroom open and walked in with Willy behind her.

"Ah, Ajan John are you looking forward to the new school year?"

"Sarah! And Willy! How lovely to see you! Yes, I am. Very much indeed. Will you both be joining us?"

"We would like to, Ajan John, but we have a rather busy schedule at the moment with a project that we started before we were last reborn. That's why we're here. Our daughter from that visit found a brooch buried in the garden of the home that has been in Willy's family for generations. It is very unusual, and I was wondering whether you could take a look at it, and perhaps give us some details…"

"Yes, John, Becky… our daughter, is absolutely besotted with it. I seem to remember my great grandmother talking about it, but that's all…"

"And my research says that all of Willy's ancestors from those days and beyond have taken on new bodies… they are scattered all over the place".

"You come from a rather industrious line then, Willy, do you?"

"I don't know, John, Sarah says that I still have The Block, but we believe that it is beginning to lift".

"OK, well, I might be able to help. Where is the piece?"

"On our daughter's dressing table…", she went silent for a short while, "in a small sky-blue box. Shall we show you?"

"Yes, fine".

"When, Ajan?"

"Now, if it is accessible".

"OK, this way, please".

∞

The three entered Becky's bedroom while the family was watching TV downstairs and approached the dresser. "That one, Ajan", said Sarah trying to be helpful, but unnecessary.

"Thank you".

"Just imagine that the box is not there, Willy".

"Oh, yes!" said John running his fingers over and through the brooch "This is quite an experience! It is rare to find something like this in this part of the world. It is made of high-grade silver, and I feel that it came from not far from here…"

"You mean Welsh silver?" asked Willy before Sarah shushed him up.

"Yes, Welsh silver", said John nevertheless. "It was mined in Cwm Ystwyth or Cwm Rheidol… Ystwyth… yes, Cwm Ystwyth, without a doubt. In the early Seventeenth Century, if I'm not mistaken… or even a little before.

"It has been around, this brooch has, and belonged to... no, that is the correct phrase, been looked after by many powerful people... women, Wise Women. Oh! at least one of whom was murdered for being a witch... she was a supporter of Gwen ferch Ellis - the first Welsh woman to be hanged for witchcraft. It was in 1594... there were only five such hangings recorded in Wales, but there were more than 100,000 elsewhere in Europe...

"She was a Healer... a Healer of men and animals and she used the power of prayer to God, and plants. It seems that this was one woman's tribute to Gwen, but it got her executed... though it has been a protection for its wearer ever since. The eyes are quite striking too, aren't they? They have been cut to reflect even the minutest ray of light... the seem to follow the viewer.

"It is a very beautiful piece, Sarah, and has a lot of local history, although I don't get anything from the eye crystals. Sorry that I can't be more helpful, but thank you for letting me see it".

∞

"I can't wait to tell Becky tomorrow!" Sarah told Willy from her armchair.

"I'm sure that she will be thrilled. That silver mine at Cwm Ystwyth is only 'down the road'! It's practically in our backyard. Perhaps, she could get more details about the eyes from the mineralogy department of Cardiff University? That's where I would have gone away..."

"Ah, but John doesn't need to take samples, he works from pure vibration, which is how he can often get history on a piece too. A jeweller couldn't tell you who had owned a piece before just by touching it!"

"Oh, no, definitely not! I wasn't criticising John, not at all. I'm sorry if I gave that impression. I was most impressed by him".

"No, I knew that you weren't, dear. I can't wait to tell her though. Shall we talk to her in her dreams, and put the idea of going to Cardiff after she's got the kids off to school?"

"I haven't done that for ages, but I remember your instructions. Let's try". From their armchairs, they both talked to Becky as if she were in the room with them, and she said that she would have the time to make the trip.

∞

While her parents were telling her about John's revelations concerning her brooch, Becky was clearing away the last of the breakfast things. "That is absolutely fascinating, but I've been thinking… perhaps it would be worth taking it to the mineralogy department at Cardiff University? I looked it up this morning. They don't call it that, they call it the Cardiff University School of Earth and Ocean Sciences. It sounds a lot grander, doesn't it. Shall we go down this morning? I don't want to make an appointment in case they say 'next week'. What do you think?"

Willy winked at Sarah and she smiled back. "I'm all for it, cariad. Lead the way!"

As Becky drove down to Cardiff, Sarah and Willy travelled with her.

"Do you have any thoughts on how the Cottage community will progress, Becky?" Sarah was again trying to ascertain how much she remembered of the Grand Plan that had been formulated before they had all been reborn.

"Not really, Mam, but I would like to set up a few community projects. We could re-instate the prison visits. I honestly think that they not only did a lot of good for the inmates, but that they helped perhaps in our village too. It helped them see that not all prisoners are all bad, and it helped them get a few extra Karma points.

"Then I think that some sort of Awareness classes would benefit the community too. Perhaps, a bit like Gareth and Emma hold in their hall. we could have guest speakers, and Development Circles too, when we have an advanced teacher amongst us. Messages from the Other Side and demonstrations always go down well too…"

"The future of the community is paramount. I think that you should concentrate on its well-being. That is not to say that what you have just mentioned is not beneficial. I think it is, but the benefit of your own local people is a good starting point. That way, people can see the use of the Cottage and then they will be all the more willing to help out in times of crises.

"You could also offer the downstairs room as a crèche, or, in the summer, the garden as a day-care centre for toddlers, if there's any call for it".

"And I remember one of the lads asking about using the garden for bonfires!" put in Willy. "The hall could be used for suitable film shows... and the house and garden for W.I. meetings!"

"Yes, why not?" added Sarah. "In fact, there is so much that you can do if you put your mind to it. However, never think that you have to do all this alone. Now that the cottage refurbishment is complete, you do not need a Steering Committee, but that will be the basis of your church committee or the Founder Members Group. Have brainstorming sessions with them, but steer them in the right direction. You are now the Steering Committee. Your job is to encourage them to come up with the ideas and to guide them in the right direction.

"That way, you will not feel the pressure to come up with new ideas too much.

How is your John behaving these days?"

"I don't know, Mam. Sometimes, I think he's accepted the fact that he won't be selling the house, and then, all of a sudden, he seems to think that he still has a chance of doing it. I don't know what he's playing at..."

"You need to get him more involved", said Willy. "You have a new direction in life, and it's at the cost of the one he had planned, if you had sold the cottage and pocketed the money. I think that he feels left out, so you need to include him... Give him things to do, make him feel like an active and valuable member of the team".

"I think that your father's right, Becky". She looked at Willy, studied him for the briefest of whiles. It wasn't that his suggestion was clever for him - he had never been a stupid man - but it was the first clear sign that she had had that The Block was lifting and that he himself was beginning to take an active role in the Cottage Project.

"We've arrived", announced Becky suddenly. She put the car in the visitors' car park, locked up and led the way inside. She quickly found the Mineralogy Department, and then went looking for 'older people', who she thought were most likely to be the lecturers. After a few requests, a helpful, middle-aged woman took them to the staff room and introduced them, before leaving them to their own devices.

Nobody seemed particularly interested when Becky tried to explain that she hoping that someone would help her identity a crystalline gemstone that she had found, until she opened her coat to reveal the quite stunning four by three inch figurine that she had pinned below it. "I have been told that the silver is Sixteenth Century and from Cwm Ystwyth, and that the crystals might be Firestone. That's flint, isn't it?"

An elderly man with white hair and fake tortoiseshell glasses, put his book down and leaned forward. As he got out of his armchair, Becky took a step towards him and unpinned her brooch

"Could I take a closer look, young lady?" he asked holding out his hand. He first stared into the cat's eyes a few minutes, and then turned the piece over several times - examining it from all angles. His colleagues were becoming visibly more interested by the minute.

"What have you got there, Horace?" asked another middle-aged woman with short hair putting on her glasses. "Anything interesting?" He didn't reply, but rubbed one of the cat's eyes with his thumbnail, and then delved into his pocket, eventually retrieving a magnifying glass. He looked at the eyes one at a time and together from several distances. Finally, he put the piece on the table, lit his pipe lighter, and examined the eyes again with the glass by the light of the flame.

"How very unusual…" he muttered, "Might I ask where you acquired this?"

"It was my great, great, great grandmother's", she said counting out the 'greats' on her fingers.

"I would say that it is chert, which is a kind of flint, which is sometimes called firestone, because of its history of being used to create sparks to light fires and flintlocks. It is most often found in chalk or marl. However, this is a very special kind of compact, microcrystalline quartz commonly called Jasper. Jasper comes in a variety of colours… sometimes even a dull red, when oxidised iron is present, but I have never, not in all my years, seen crimson Jasper - the colour of fresh blood. It is remarkable, quite remarkable, and, in my opinion, completely unique.

"As to its provenance…, well… it is impossible to tell… If there are no other examples, it really could have come from anywhere… literally anywhere… it could even have fallen out of the sky on a meteorite.

"I don't suppose you would permit me to carry out some tests on it - non-destructive, of course?"

"Er, no, Professor Williams", she said reading his ID tag. "I couldn't possibly let you do that. I feel as if he's, Jasper is part of the family, but thank you very much for your help".

As Becky turned to go, she saw the other teachers gathering around Professor Williams, bombarding him with questions. "Er, miss, before you go. Might I take a photograph of Jasper, and have a contact number too, in case I come up with anything else?"

Becky allowed the photograph, and gave the professor her name and number before hurrying away elated.

Her parents were astonished by the news too.

Life in Annwn

Glossary

Bryn: hill
Cariad: love, lover, sweetheart, dear.
Coupy: squat
Kiddy: from *ci du* – Welsh for black dog (cŵn=dogs).
Teg: fair
Twp: crazy, mad
Y Tylwyth Teg: The Fair Family; The Fair People; the Fairies

Life in Annwn

Bonus chapter

First chapter of the sequel:

LEAVING ANNWN

Returning to Earth on a Mission!

by

Owen Jones

CHAPTER ONE: AN EVENING STROLL

"The place looks so different these days, doesn't it, Sarah?"

"Yes, my dear… life seems dismal and disappointing to so many people. I haven't seen such a general feeling of depression since the time of the Great Plague. It is so sad, Willy".

"Mmm, 'The Black Death'… So many of us worked for so long to help relieve the suffering in those days, but it seemed so much easier back then. There was more, er hope, I suppose than in these days".

"People had more strongly-held religious beliefs in the 14th Century even though between seventy-five and two hundred million people died.

Although many of the religious leaders were hypocrites, the people really did believe in God and an Afterlife. It's not the same any more. People find it dispiriting to think that the daily grind is all there is to life".

"Not only has work become less-well paid for most people, but there is a lot of uncertainty with Zero-Hours Contracts, firms going bankrupt and impoverished Social Services. Many people are not only working longer hours, or having two jobs, but they are still worse off than ten years ago. The poor and the needy feel abandoned and ripped-off by the State and the rich people who run it".

"Winter is beginning to set in, yet look at all the people begging and even sleeping on the streets, Sarah!"

"Christmas is on its way, but the place reminds me more of a city of refugees on the edge of a battle zone".

"There has not been such a financial discrepancy between the Have's and the Have-not's in Britain since the Victorian Era, but like I said, people had more religious belief – more hope – in those days. Mankind is in this sad state of affairs despite the massive effort Spirit is making to help people see The Truth".

"Sarah, there are Spirit Guides and Helpers everywhere, but so few of these poor people realise that they are never really alone especially when times are rough. No matter how long I do this work, it still gets to me. How long has it been now? Do you remember? You're better at dates than I am".

"You passed away thirty-three years ago, and you started helping right away, because you recovered from your life on Earth so quickly".

"Thirty-three years ago! Sometimes, it seems much longer and yet, at other times, the period has flown past. I know that providing comfort to the afflicted is necessary and worthwhile, but... it can be so depressing too. Yes, I hate to say it, but sometimes, it cheeses me off that so few people actually listen when I talk to them. It makes me want to pack it all in... sometimes, just sometimes".

"Many of us feel like that from time to time, Willy, but you have to keep your eyes on the long term. Even if you only get through to a few

Souls, those people will tell others and word gets around that there is Life After Death. Every single one that you remind that reincarnation exists could rekindle the light in dozens of others".

"I know, I know! That's the only thing that keeps me going most of the time".

"Well, it is true that not all of us see a project through to the end… a few Spirit Guides give up on their charges for one reason or another…"

"I, for one, am not surprised, it is demoralising when you are constantly trying to talk with someone, but they never, never ever seem to be listening!"

"I know, but it's usually not because they are not listening, but because they cannot hear you. Spirit Guides that give up should never have been selected for the job in truth though".

"OK, I can see that, but there are those living on The Surface who do know about their Spirit Guides, but still refuse to listen!"

"Yes, there are those too, but you always have to remember that everyone - 'Dead or Alive', so to speak, has free choice. No-one can force anyone to do or believe anything. Persuasion is the name of the game, and some people are just not very persuasive, but there are many other types of work that those people can do, as you well know".

"Like working with animals, you mean?"

"Amongst others, yes. You still enjoy working with abused and neglected animals, don't you?"

"Yes, of course I do, Sarah! You know, I do, but then animals are aware of us – it is more satisfying, as far as that goes".

"Yes, however, you are talking to the converted when you're dealing with animals. It is more challenging to work with humans, and ultimately, more rewarding too, but I agree that the work doesn't suit everyone. You have… are doing well, but perhaps direct contact with people is not really your forte, which is why being a shepherd suited you so well".

"Oh, I'm not giving up! It's just that I understand how disheartening it can be for some. It is not an easy job, Yes, it is rewarding to see someone notice you, but it happens so infrequently these days".

Life in Annwn

"This is indeed an extremely materialistic period in time, perhaps, the most materialistic ever. There are forces at work encouraging materialism because it suits their Earthly goals. These are very rich, selfish, amoral people, who will go to any lengths to grab more money and more power for themselves to the cost of anyone… However, they are Spirit too, so even with them, there is a chance that they will see The Light.

"I'll tell you something. If you think that working to help the poor and needy is difficult, try making the rich and greedy change their ways. That really is depressing!"

"I can imagine, and I know you try, Sarah. I couldn't do it, I despise the super greedy… and I know that that's wrong too, but I can't help it".

"No, not yet, my darling, but I know that you can see that if even one as advanced as yourself can't stomach the super selfish, then it is not surprising that many of those who need our help can't see us too… and there are people working on you too to help you get over your prejudice against the super greedy".

"I know. People like you, for a start… and our Becky. She is so much like you".

"We have worked together for a very long time… many centuries before we decided that she should be born our daughter on The Surface and that we should become an Earthly team".

"I remember you telling me that before, and I believe you, of course, but I never have understood how that useless husband of hers, er, John, wasn't it, fitted into the picture".

"Oh, John is one of Becky's most promising students, but he was worried about being reborn on The Surface again, so Becky offered to allow him to join up with her on Earth to help him settle in. He did his best, love".

"I suppose so. Not my type either though, I'm afraid".

"He vibrates at a different – OK, lower – level to you. That's why, and you know that, so you ought to try harder. And while we're on the subject, that is why you can't stomach the super greedy too – they just vibrate far too low beneath you. There is no resonance… you and they are out of harmony in the most basic of ways. The discord is so great that you cannot bear their company. They are mostly too base to understand you on that level, but they hate the things you say, which represent everything that makes them feel uneasy. People like you make them feel uncomfortable, so they retaliate against you – even try to hurt you.

"You need to learn to rise above that, because they can only hurt your physical body. Still, all in good time, eh? Walking through the centre of Cardiff after nightfall really is like being in a war zone, isn't it?" said Sarah as they walked up the shopping precinct called Queen Street towards Cardiff Castle, suspended a foot off the ground.

"This is the most prosperous area of the city with its symbols of power – the government buildings and the castle – and yet look around us… it seems 'cold' too – impersonal, unhelpful, and unyielding… It will get much colder in temperature too over the coming months, before it becomes warmer again. I suppose many of the poor sods we see here will be back with us in Annwn by then though".

"They aren't 'poor sods', Willy, as well you know! They chose to be reborn to follow a course that interested them when they were in Annwn. It just so happens that these Dark Times are conducive to learning harsh lessons and many people are taking advantage of it".

"Yes, I know. They actually came to The Surface to learn how to deal with sleeping on the streets…"

"Well, among many other things, yes, but that is one of the hardest lessons to learn. Not sleeping on the streets, I mean, but remembering that we chose our course on Earth ourselves before we came back up here".

"It is hard to tell people that they are being blown up or sleeping rough because they chose to though, isn't it?"

"Yes, and it is hard to remember that the super rich and greedy have chosen to play those rôles in their university course on The Surface too… they are only acting out a part in a play".

"OK, point taken. I even know it and have done for as long as I can remember, but I cannot keep the idea in the front of my mind".

"It is very difficult, my dear, but then being 'dead' doesn't make you an angel, does? Deciding to study the Laws is one thing, but it is another to actually remember them, AND then it takes lifetimes to learn how to live by them".

"I know, but we will all get there in the end".

"You could express it that way, although I prefer to think of it as 'as one day', because there is no end that I know of… eternity is infinite, surely?"

"I can't argue with that, Sarah. One thing I do know, is that I am so glad that I have you on my side. I am a very lucky man. You know, I never get tired of talking to you – even when you are trying to teach me. That has to be a sign of a top educator, but I have always known that you are far more advanced than I. I even knew it when we were married in our little cottage on the Brecon Beacons and I kept you so busy that you were virtually housebound. I was cruel to you, but you never complained, you just got on with your work and held our family together".

"You couldn't hear what I used to say about you when you were in the pub!", she laughed.

"Perhaps, but I'm not sure that I believe you on that score… You were always my guiding light, and I knew it even then, although I had forgotten that I had known you before in Annwn. Did you remember Annwn before we married on The Surface?"

"No, I can't say that I did. I didn't really know about Annwn then either. I called it Heaven like everyone else did, but I did feel a strong attraction to the mountains I could see out of our back kitchen window… beyond our back garden. I would talk to them when I was doing the washing-up or the laundry. I loved being in our garden most of all though. It made me feel free. I knew that you and Kiddy were on our little mountain tending the sheep not far away, and I wanted to be out there too".

"I'm sorry for being such a pig, my darling".

"You have said that many times since, Willy, and I know you mean it. I knew it wasn't the real you doing it then too, you were only doing what you needed to do to get through the day. You were a good husband during hard times, and you never went astray or left us wanting".

"They were hard times, but I can't help thinking that these are even harder than then. Despite the religious aspect, we grew up after the Great Depression and the Second World War, they were times of great hope for the future. That hope is lacking now, sadly lacking, you might say.

"Money is scarce…"

"It always has been for people like us!"

"Yes, but our generation could buy our own homes, kids these days can't. We could travel… well, not you and me, because of the sheep, but it was easy because of the European Union, but kids now have seen that dragged away from them too. Not only that, but we could retire at sixty-five and the youth of today will have to work until they are seventy or even seventy-five. We had the chance of free university too, or our Becky did, and now even that's gone! Expensive further education, low wages, difficult travel and rented accommodation – that's what our kids lave to look forward to… AND and extra ten years of work.

"I'm not surprised they're angry, me!"

"No, I know you're not. You have a good heart… but a poor memory. Those kids, as you keep calling them, are taking advantage of the current times to learn the lessons that it has to offer, and they include hardship. Which is something the poor, or the relatively poor, have always had to bear, even in this rich country. It is much worse in most other countries, don't forget".

"I know, I know, but I cannot help feeling that it is not right…"

"Well, it is right, otherwise those courses would not be available at this beautiful university that we call Earth".

"I know, I do know, really. You are right, I know you are, but I still cannot live that lesson".

"You will, Willy, one day, you will – everyone will - but knowing it and living it are totally different kettles of fish. Let me give you a kiss, you great big softie. Have you had enough? Do you want to go home, my dear?"

"I have had enough, and I do want to go home, my dear. You can read my Aura, but you would know anyway… you know me better than I know myself, but I want to walk and talk a little longer. I want to learn the lessons you try to teach me… I want to be a successful student… to make you proud of me".

"Please don't talk like that, my love. I am proud of you. I always have been, and I cannot imagine that there will ever come a day when I will not be, but it is good for you to progress. You know what is right, but, as you yourself say, you cannot accept what you know, or, in your own words, you cannot yet live that life. Your beloved kids would probably say that you can talk the talk, but not yet walk the walk", she said smiling into his face. Willy put his arms around his wife and kissed her.

"You always know just what to say", he said squeezing her again and releasing her.

"We should be lending a hand, I suppose", said Willy taking Sarah's hand and walking on.

"Only if we want to", she replied. "We are allowed to have time to ourselves too. There is no-one to say what anyone has to do or should be doing. No-one will ever criticise us even if we never help anyone ever again. You know that too".

"Yes, but there are those who would be very surprised if you packed it all in and went to live on a deserted paradise planet, aren't there?"

"Yes, I suppose there are!" she laughed, "but that sort of life wouldn't suit you either, would it? Not in the long run. You and I are very much alike. We want to help… to make a difference… and what we, and the countless of millions of other Spirit Guides, do, does make a difference. You know it does. You could no more sit on a paradise island for the rest of Eternity than I could".

"No, I guess you're right again, but I am a bit world-weary tonight, and don't have the strength to help at the moment, so can we just walk and watch?"

"Of course! However, that's helping too, or it could be. What if one of these late-night shoppers saw us kissing just now? He or she would tell his or her family and friends and that would start people talking about ghosts and life after death, which is what we want – to spark thought".

"We could become a legend – 'The Kissing Ghost Couple of Queen Street'!"

"Oh, yes! 'But then we would have to come back and do it again on a regular basis – what day is it today? Every Friday night, or every third week in October", she giggled.

"I'd be happy to come back here every night, if it meant a kiss from you".

"What, in the line of duty, you mean?"

"No, in the line of preference... You always were better at words than me".

" I was only joking. Ooh, you are getting maudlin, aren't you? Is all this misery getting to you again?"

"I suppose it is. Sorry, my dear. I should have known you were only joking... and if I didn't know, I should have looked at your Aura".

"You are run down, and you are taking all this to heart", she said squeezing his hand with her right hand and indicating the rough sleepers with her left.

"Yes, you are right, as always, my love, but I really don't want to go home just yet. Let's walk past St. John The Baptist Church and into St. Mary Street. I love that little church – it's Fifteenth Century, I think. It's like an island of Goodness in the surrounding shopping centre of Babylon".

"I know what you mean. I like it too". There was a trestle table outside the small isolated church, where two women and a man were handing out mugs of hot soup ladled from a huge tureen to anyone who asked for some. There was a pile of bread rolls to dip in it too, but no spoons as they had all been stolen on previous evenings. Diners were using their own mugs, which meant that most of the thick pea and ham soup went to those for whom it was intended and not to hungry shoppers. It also satisfied the current anti Covid-19 measures of not sharing cutlery or utensils, which could be used as a reason for not serving just anyone who felt peckish.

"That is a heart-warming sight, isn't it, Sarah? I'm glad that I saw that tonight before going home".

"Look!" said Sarah, pointing to one of the women with her chin and smiling. "That lady there can see us, but she can hardly believe her eyes. Let's give her a big wave and cheery smile". Willy looked over and did as he was bid. The young woman's mouth dropped open as she tried to signal to her colleagues what she could see. Willy and Sarah waited a minute to see whether the others would be able to see them as well, but moved on when it became obvious that they could not.

"Yes, that has made my day!" said Willy.

"Many people are trying to help, Willy, not only Spirit, although many Surface Dwellers are inspired by Spirit, even if they are well-intentioned anyway. Like those people back there. I looked for a banner to advertise their organisation, but didn't see one. They probably weren't looking for recognition… they just wanted to help".

"Oh, I'm sure that there are people who just want to help. Definitely… In fact, we knew some in the village, didn't we? Er, um… I forget their names now, but there definitely were".

"Yes, sure there were. There are nice people everywhere. Most of them just need a little nudge in the right direction so that they know that they are not alone. Does that sound familiar? We provide the nudge from our side to those who can see us, and they provide the same sort of nudge to people on their side. We are all working to alleviate suffering; the main difference being that they try to improve lives one day, or even one meal at a time, and we try to change whole lives, or outlooks. We try to teach that there is nothing to fear but fear itself, and that no-one can really harm you because of Life After Death and Re-incarnatiom".

"I imagine that sometimes a warm meal on a cold night is of more help".

"In the sort term, probably so, but it is like a glutton going on a diet. They soon put the weight back on. However, if you teach them to love exercise, or how much they are damaging the planet, you may change their way of life for ever so that they can give up dieting. It's the same with compulsive shoppers… and drinkers… most addicts, in fact. They all go for the quick fix to their obsession rather than finding out why they are unhappy and fixing the reason for that instead.

"People treat symptoms instead of curing the illness, and so the problem keeps recurring, requiring another dose of what the patient is addicted to, and then another… ad infinitum, until they meet and listen to, someone like us". Sarah smiled. She was not being sanctimonious or self-righteous, she was simply stating The Truth.

"Yes, my darling, well, we can all only do our best, and at the moment I feel dead beat. I think I am ready to go home now and call it a day. Unless you want to carry on…"

"No, no, I can go back too. Tomorrow is another day, and we are not so close to our goal that finishing up for the day will make any difference. Besides, there are many more people still continuing the Good Fight. No, let's just go back home. Ready? One, two, three!"

They were instantaneously standing in their small apartment above the cottage where they had spent all their married life on the small mountain that they called their own. The ground floor of the cottage was a Spiritualist Sanctuary and a village Community Centre now, but they had left the attic so that the donors of the building could use it as a refuge. Willy and Sarah had been using it for this purpose for three decades and Becky sometimes stayed there too. They preferred it to the hustle and bustle of the city of Annwn, or even the quiet of the surrounding countryside. It was their own little cottage, and they were its resident ghosts, whom most of the people who used the building regularly had seen several times.

"It has been a good day", said Sarah, "so you have reason to be worn out. Let's go and lie down to recharge our batteries".

"I'm ready for that", replied Willy as they disappeared into their bedroom and appeared on the bed. The room had all their old furniture, or at least all the items that meant anything to them, although whether they had been there or not would not have mattered to them, as they could easily conjure up anything that they needed or wanted. It had been their daughter Becky's idea to put their stuff in their flat, and they hadn't had the heart to say 'No'. Kiddy, their old sheep dog bounded up onto the bed at their feet.

"There's a good girl, Kiddy", murmured Willy sleepily. "Good night, girl. Good night to you too, Sarah. Let's see what tomorrow brings".

They didn't need to sleep in the way that Surface Dwellers had to – they didn't have bodies that needed rest, but they did need time out. They felt the need to plug into the Universe from time to time, but not necessarily every day. They would usually go their separate ways when they 'rested', but not always, and they didn't always go anywhere.

Rest to them was more like a meditation; a time to gather their thoughts; a time to strengthen their own individual inner peace.

About the Author

Author Owen Jones, from Barry, South Wales, came to writing novels relatively recently, although he has been writing all his adult life. He has lived and worked in several countries and travelled in many, many more.

He speaks, or has spoken, seven languages fluently and is currently learning Thai, since he lives in Thailand with his Thai wife of ten years.

"It has never taken me long to learn a language", he says, "but Thai bears no relationship to any other language I have ever studied before."

When asked about his style of writing, he said, "I'm a Celt, and we are Romantic. I believe in reincarnation and lots more besides in that vein. Those beliefs, like 'Do unto another…', and 'What goes round comes around', Fate and Karma are central to my life, so they are reflected in my work'.

His first novel, 'Daddy's Hobby' from the series 'Behind The Smile: The Story of Lek, a Bar Girl in Pattaya' has been followed by four sequels, but his largest collection is 'The Megan Series', eighteen novellas on the psychic development of a young teenage girl, the subtitle of which, 'A Spirit Guide, A Ghost Tiger and One Scary Mother!' sums them up nicely.

As Owen puts it:

> 'Born in the Land of Song,
> living in the Land of Smiles'.

Life in Annwn

Owen Jones

Other Books by the Same Author

Behind The Smile:
The Story of Lek, a Bar Girl in Pattaya
Daddy's Hobby
An Exciting Future
Maya – Illusion
The Lady in the Tree
Stepping Stones
The Dream
The Beginning

-

The Disallowed
Chupacabras on Backpacker Blood-Milkshake

-

Tiger Lily of Bangkok
When the Seeds of Revenge Blossom!
Tiger Lily of Bangkok in London
The Tiger Re-awakens!

-

Alien House
A Story of Love, Despair, and Alien Intervention!

-

Andropov's Cuckoo
A story of Love, Intrigue, and The KGB!

-

Life in Annwn

A Night in Annwn
The Strange Story of Old Willy Jones' Near-Death Experience

Life in Annwn
The Story of Willy Jones' Life in Heaven

Leaving Annwn
Leaving Annwn on a Mission

-

Fate Twister
The Story of Wayne Gamm

-

Dead Centre
Not Every Suicide-Bomber Is Religious!

Dead Centre 2
Even The Wrong Can Be Right Sometimes!

-

Alien House
A Story of Love, Hope and Alien Intervention

-

Daisy's Chain
A Story of Love, Intrigue and The Underworld on The Costa del Sol

-

The Bull at the Gate
The day the Sky Fell!

-

Owen Jones

The Psychic Megan Series
A Spirit Guide, A Ghost Tiger, and One Scary Mother!
The Misconception
Megan's Thirteenth
Megan's School Trip
Megan's School Exams
Megan's Followers
Megan and the Lost Cat
Megan and the Mayoress
Megan Faces Derision
Megan's Grandparents' Visit
Megan's Father Falls Ill
Megan Goes on Holiday
Megan and the Burglar
Megan and the Cyclist
Megan and the Old Lady
Megan's Garden
Megan Goes to the Zoo
Megan Goes Hiking
Megan and the W. I. Cookery Competition
Megan Goes Riding
Megan and the Radio One Beach Party
Megan Goes Yachting
Megan At Carnival
Megan's Christmas
Megan Catches Covid-19

Life in Annwn

Non-Fiction:

How to Give Your Dog a Real Dog's Life
and make him love you for it!

The Eternal Plan
– Revealed
(written by Colin Jones, compiled by Owen Jones)

Authorship
Publishing Your Book On You Own

For more information about my books, please visit my blog at: https://meganpublishingservices.com

Please leave a review of this book and series where you bought it from, and consider keeping in touch with me on your favourite social media platform.
My contact details are in this book.
Best wishes, and thank you for reading my story,
Owen

www.ingramcontent.com/pod-product-compliance
Lightning Source LLC
Chambersburg PA
CBHW070600010526
44118CB00012B/1397